MW01631055

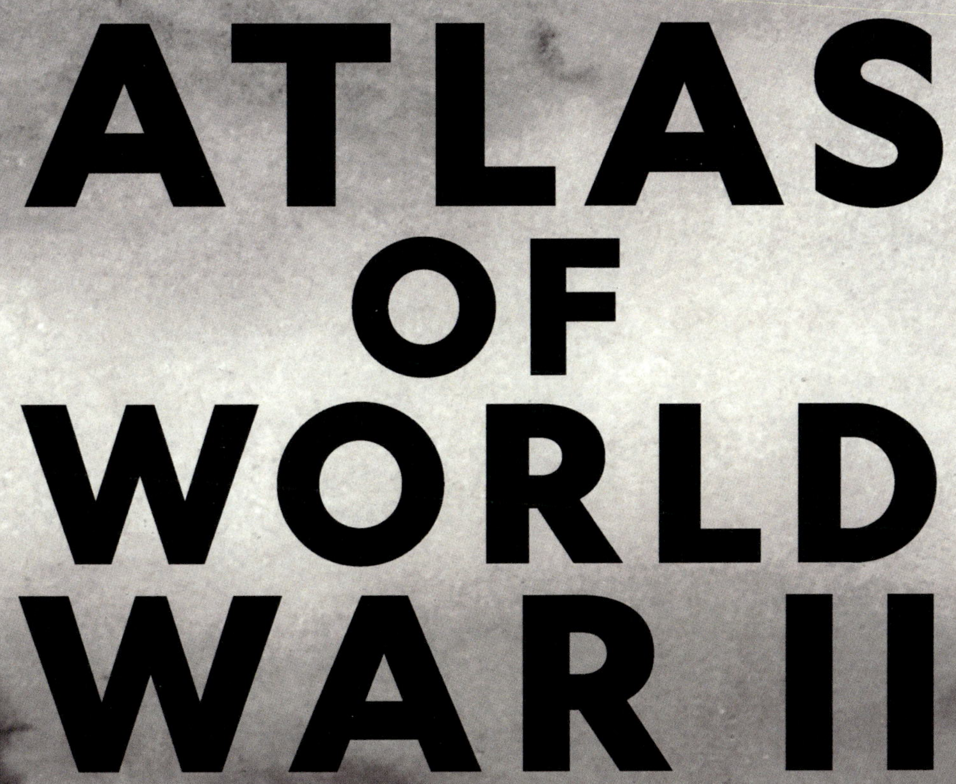

ATLAS OF WORLD WAR II

EXPLORE HISTORY'S GREATEST CONFLICT

NATIONAL GEOGRAPHIC

WASHINGTON, D.C.

CONTENTS

COVER: **A barrier of linked fortresses shielded German-occupied territory against Allied invasion. D-Day landings targeted Normandy, which was less heavily defended than Calais.** PREVIOUS PAGES: **American Boeing B-24 Liberators of the U.S. 15th Air Force bomb oil refineries at Ploesti, Romania—a major source of fuel for the German war effort—on August 1, 1943.** LEFT: **Soldiers of the U.S. 37th Infantry Division fire from behind a Sherman tank at Japanese troops on the Pacific island of Bougainville in early 1944.**

CAROLINE ISLANDS
MARSHALL ISLANDS
CAROLINE AND MARSHALL ISLANDS
PALAU ISLANDS
KUSAIE
JALUIT
MARIANAS ISLANDS
ROTA
GUAM
GILBERT ISLANDS
ELLICE ISLANDS
BISMARCK ARCHIPELAGO
SANTA CRUZ ISLANDS
TORRES AND BANKS ISLANDS
U. S. S. R.
RUSSIAN SOCIALIST FEDERATED SOVIET REPUBLIC
BERING SEA
SEA OF OKHOTSK
ALEUTIAN ISLANDS
GULF OF ALASKA
NORTH PACIFIC OCEAN
SEA OF JAPAN
CHINA
INDIA
BURMA
PHILIPPINES
NETHERLANDS INDIES
Japanese Mandate
Australian Mandate
Great Britain
United States Great Britain
New Zealand
France
AUSTRALIA
CORAL SEA
SOUTH PACIFIC
TASMAN SEA
NEW ZEALAND
NORTH ISLAND
SOUTH ISLAND
TASMANIA
INDIAN OCEAN
PACIFIC
AIRLINE DISTANCES IN STATUTE MILES
LEEWARD GROUP (ILES SOUS LE VENT)
TAHITI AND MOOREA
PAPEETE
ILES DE LA SOCIÉTÉ
GAMBIER ISLANDS
MAKATEA

NATIONAL GEOGRAPHIC'S WARTIME MAPS

When America entered World War II in 1942, the demand for maps of battle zones was filled not only by government agencies but also by the National Geographic Society. The Society's trusted maps proved useful to many officers, including the commander of the Pacific Fleet. In September 1942, Adm. Chester Nimitz was flying to Guadalcanal when the pilot of their B-17 lost his way in bad weather. The pilot's small-scale chart of the Solomons showed only the larger islands. Nimitz related, "It was our good fortune that the Marine officer on my staff followed the practice of always carrying a National Geographic map in his briefcase." Shown at left, it included an inset of the Solomons detailing the smaller and larger islands. Flying low, they recognized islands off San Cristobal, and made it to Henderson Field, where Nimitz conferred a medal on Lt. Col. Evans Carlson. In a postwar letter to Gilbert Grosvenor, president of the National Geographic Society, Nimitz stated that his flight to Guadalcanal was one of many occasions "when your maps proved invaluable to the forces in the Pacific." These maps, retrieved from the Society's archives in Washington, D.C., along with others on these pages, give us insightful perspectives on a world at war—from day-to-day decisions to long-term strategies that determined the outcome of World War II. ■

LEFT: **During the war, the National Geographic Society gave both President Franklin D. Roosevelt and Prime Minister Winston Churchill wall-mounted cabinets filled with maps to locate far-flung theaters of battle such as the Pacific islands.**

This top secret map of Omaha Beach was created thanks to daring coastal and aerial reconnaissance. During the D-Day invasion of Normandy on June 6, 1944, the beach-masters relied on the notations in red to locate German beach obstacles, mines, and other defenses.

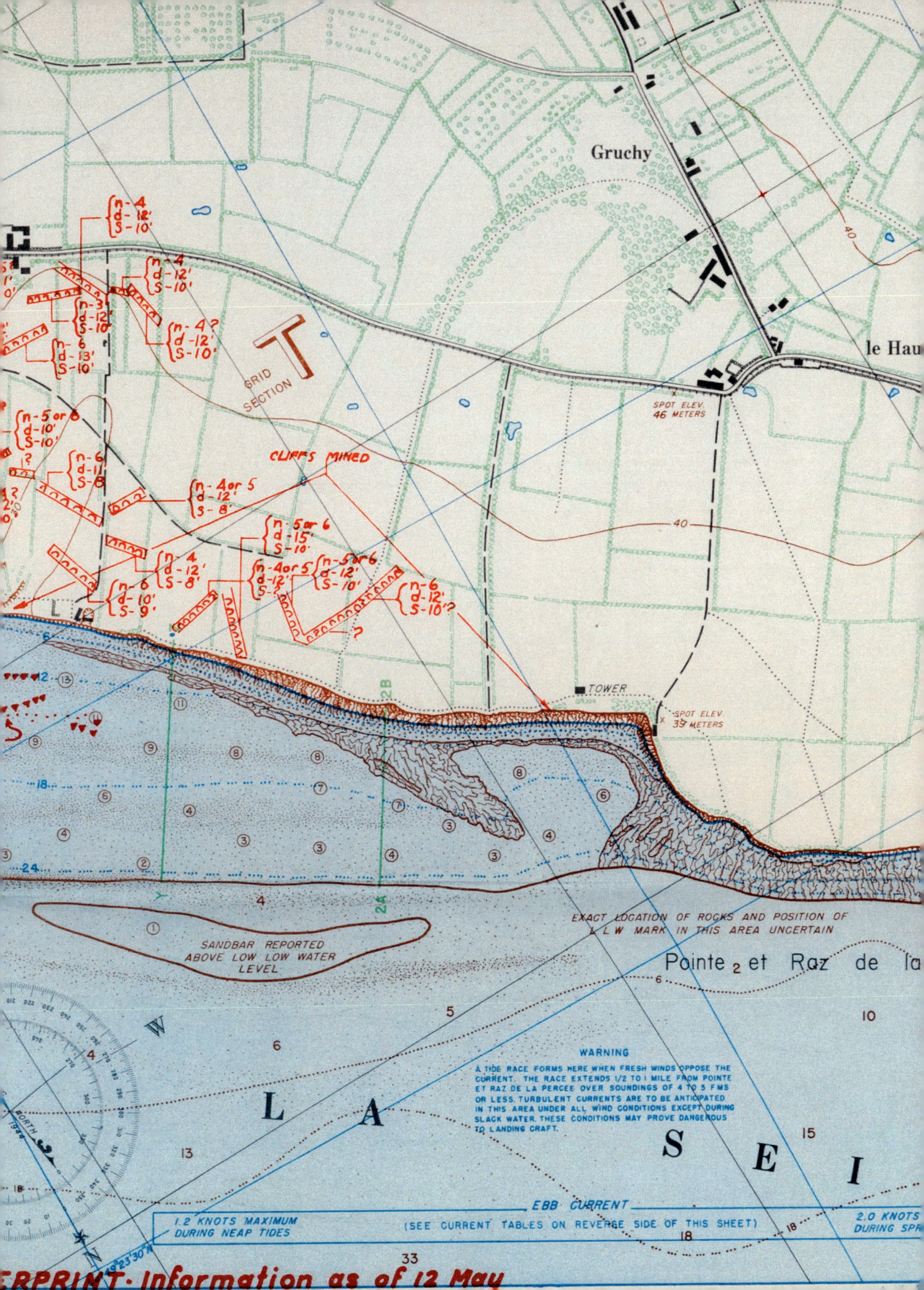

Gruchy
le Hau
GRID SECTION
CLIFFS MINED
SPOT ELEV. 46 METERS
TOWER
SPOT ELEV. 39 METERS
EXACT LOCATION OF ROCKS AND POSITION OF L L W MARK IN THIS AREA UNCERTAIN
Pointe et Raz de la
SANDBAR REPORTED ABOVE LOW LOW WATER LEVEL
WARNING
A TIDE RACE FORMS HERE WHEN FRESH WINDS OPPOSE THE CURRENT. THE RACE EXTENDS 1/2 TO 1 MILE FROM POINTE ET RAZ DE LA PERCEE OVER SOUNDINGS OF 4 TO 5 FMS OR LESS. TURBULENT CURRENTS ARE TO BE ANTICIPATED IN THIS AREA UNDER ALL WIND CONDITIONS EXCEPT DURING SLACK WATER. THESE CONDITIONS MAY PROVE DANGEROUS TO LANDING CRAFT.
L A S E I
EBB CURRENT
1.2 KNOTS MAXIMUM DURING NEAP TIDES
(SEE CURRENT TABLES ON REVERSE SIDE OF THIS SHEET)
2.0 KNOTS DURING SPR
RPRINT · Information as of 12 May

Invading German soldiers race through a blazing Norwegian village in April 1940, as World War II ignites.

CHAPTER 1

SETTING EUROPE ABLAZE

PRELUDE TO WAR–1941

The armistice that ended the Great War left many Germans bitterly resentful, including Adolf Hitler. In 1923, Hitler led a revolt that earned him political notoriety though it proved unsuccessful and landed him in jail, where he composed his manifesto, *Mein Kampf* (My Struggle). The text demonized those he blamed for subverting the German Reich, notably revolutionaries, Communists, and Jews. He became chancellor of Germany in 1933, before seizing power as the nation's Führer (leader).

In defiance of the restrictions of the Treaty of Versailles, Hitler expanded the military in preparation to wage war against his Allied foes and also against German Jews, whom Nazis assailed in an anti-Semitic outburst of violence on November 9, 1938, which became known as Kristallnacht—the Night of Broken Glass. By mid-1939, Hitler had annexed Austria and occupied Czechoslovakia. After failing to appease him, British and French leaders pledged to fight if Poland was attacked.

To avoid another long, exhausting war, German commanders launched a blitzkrieg (lightning war), led by armored units supported by the Luftwaffe, the Reich's formidable air force. Such tactics crushed Poland, swept through the Low Countries, and conquered France with staggering speed. Yet Britain defied invasion and withstood the Luftwaffe's punishing air raids, and Hitler was forced to suspend plans for a full-scale invasion of the island nation. In June 1941, Germany turned against Soviet dictator Joseph Stalin, breaking their secret pact of nonaggression. But Hitler's forces were driven back from Moscow and soon faced a prolonged war of the sort that had sunk the Reich in 1918.

1914–1918
World War I pitches Germany, Austria-Hungary, and the Ottoman Empire against France, Great Britain, and Russia (and later the U.S.).

JUNE 28, 1919
The Treaty of Versailles imposes stringent peace terms on Germany.

OCTOBER 24, 1929
The stock market crash in the U.S. triggers the Great Depression, causing global economic turmoil.

JANUARY 30, 1933
Hitler becomes chancellor of Germany.

MARCH 12, 1938
Hitler annexes Austria.

SEPTEMBER 30, 1938
British and French leaders yield to Hitler at Munich, allowing him to seize the Sudetenland in Czechoslovakia.

NOVEMBER 9–10, 1938
Nazis attack Jewish homes, businesses, and synagogues on Kristallnacht (the Night of Broken Glass).

AUGUST 23, 1939
Germany and the Soviet Union sign a nonaggression pact.

SEPTEMBER 1, 1939
German forces invade Poland, leading France and Britain to declare war.

FROM A GREAT WAR TO A GLOBAL CONFLICT

+++++++++++++

The "war to end all wars," the ruinous conflict that ended in 1918, was actually a tragic precursor to the global catastrophe that erupted in 1939. World War I began in 1914 as a struggle between the Central Powers of Germany, Austria-Hungary, and the Ottoman Empire, and the Allied Powers of Britain, France, and Russia, joined by Italy in 1915 and the U.S. in 1917. The war extended to colonies in Africa and Asia, but it was waged largely in Europe. After German forces were stopped short of Paris, both sides dug in, and the ensuing trench warfare resulted in horrendous losses. Millions died in a prolonged stalemate, and only late in the war did Allied advances finally force the collapse of the Central Powers.

The 1919 Treaty of Versailles established the League of Nations but failed to stabilize a fractured continent. Germany was forced to pay reparations and was allowed only a skeletal army of 100,000 men and no air force—terms that stoked the resentments of veterans like Adolf Hitler. British prime minister David Lloyd George warned that if Germany felt unduly punished, "she would find means of exacting retribution from her conquerors." Italy felt slighted after gaining little at Versailles to satisfy its imperial ambitions. WWI shattered the German, Austro-Hungarian, and Ottoman Empires, and it left new nations such as Czechoslovakia and Yugoslavia vulnerable. Postwar economic chaos left millions susceptible to the appeals of fascist strongmen like Benito Mussolini and Hitler, who exploited the turmoil caused by hyperinflation in the early 1920s and the Great Depression a decade later. By the late 1930s, Hitler and Mussolini had defied the Treaty of Versailles, and the victory of totalitarian ruler Gen. Francisco Franco in the Spanish Civil War foreshadowed a second world war that would surpass the dreadful toll of the first. ■

ABOVE: **A crashed plane in France during World War I**

The defeat of the Central Powers in 1918 shattered national borders in Europe. New nations such as Czechoslovakia and Yugoslavia were internally divided and vulnerable to invasion. Poland was reconstituted and waged war to avoid being reabsorbed by Russia under Vladimir Lenin, whose Soviet forces crushed Ukraine's bid for independence. By the 1930s, Poland was in a precarious position between Stalin's Soviet Union and Hitler's Germany; the Führer hoped to annex ethnically German lands such as Austria and the Polish Corridor. Hitler also intended to reoccupy the Rhineland and had designs on Alsace-Lorraine, which France had reacquired from Germany in 1919.

THE NAZI DEATH CULT

As Hitler rose to power, the Nazi Party fostered a nationalistic cult that demanded unquestioning loyalty to the Führer and taught followers to fulfill their destiny as a master race by dehumanizing others. Thousands were held spellbound by Hitler's rhetoric at large rallies. Boys in the Hitler Youth took military training and imbibed Nazi propaganda. The Nazi League of German Girls stressed physical fitness, but the imperative was to bear healthy children to bolster Hitler's expansive Reich.

Children with deformities or mental impairment were sent to institutions, where, after 1939, "defective" inmates were killed. Some perished in gas chambers, a method later used to annihilate millions. Hitler's death cult was enforced by the SS. Its chief, Heinrich Himmler, expounded Nazi racial dogma, which divided society into the "superhumans" of the Aryan master race, "subhumans" like the Slavs who inhabited much of Eastern Europe, and "antihumans," a label applied to those who were Jewish, homosexual, and Romany (Gypsy) as a pretext for extermination. Racial obsessions reinforced Hitler's determination to invade Poland and Russia, where Slavs would be displaced to make room for Germans; Jews and Romany would be exterminated; and the global movement Hitler called "Jewish Bolshevism" would be rooted out.

WAR IN THE EAST

++++++++++++++

The stage was set for World War II in August 1939, when Hitler and Stalin concluded a nonaggression pact. A secret protocol divided Eastern Europe into German and Soviet spheres of influence, which enabled Hitler to seize most of Poland and allowed Stalin to occupy eastern Poland and target Finland and the Baltic states. The pact was a blow to French and British leaders, who had opened negotiations with Russia for an alliance against Germany but could not overcome their distrust of Stalin, notorious for his murderous purges. Hitler had no such qualms about the Soviet dictator, whose regime he intended to destroy in due time.

Hitler wiped Poland off the map by invading on September 1, 1939, using German-controlled Slovakia as a staging ground. Closely supported by Stuka dive-bombers, Nazi troops invaded on several fronts (see map opposite). Army Group North, led by Gen. Fedor von Bock, delivered twin blows in conjunction with Gen. Georg von Küchler's Third Army, which advanced south from East Prussia, and Gen. Günther von Kluge's Fourth Army, which pushed east across the Polish Corridor to seize Danzig before pivoting toward Warsaw. Army Group South, under Gen. Gerd von Rundstedt, applied further pressure as Gen. Johannes Blaskowitz's Eighth Army and Gen. Walter von Reichenau's 10th Army advanced from southeastern Germany while Gen. Wilhelm List's 14th Army invaded from Slovakia and took Krakow. German tanks and motorized infantry punched through Polish forces, whose outdated cavalry offered no defense. Within a week, German armored units were approaching Warsaw.

LEFT: **In a scene reminiscent of WWI, ill-fated Polish cavalrymen train for battle before the German invasion in 1939.**

THE FALL OF WARSAW

In mid-September, as mapped, Army Group North enveloped Warsaw's eastern flank while the Eighth

German troops invaded Poland on several fronts in early September 1939. Army Group North delivered twin blows by Gen. Georg von Küchler's Third Army, which advanced south from East Prussia, and Gen. Günther von Kluge's Fourth Army, which pushed east to seize Danzig before pivoting toward Warsaw. Army Group South, under Gen. Gerd von Rundstedt, applied further pressure as Gen. Johannes Blaskowitz's Eighth Army and Gen. Walter von Reichenau's 10th Army advanced from southeastern Germany while Gen. Wilhelm List's 14th Army invaded from Germany and Slovakia and took Krakow. Warsaw would fall by the end of the month.

Army closed in from the west. Bruising assaults by German infantrymen, combined with air raids and artillery bombardments, forced the surrender of the capital on the 27th and sealed Poland's fate. Much of Poland now suffered a brutal German occupation while the rest came under Soviet domination.

Britain and France declared war on Germany yet the dreaded air attack was slow to come and few direct clashes erupted. But French troops did little more than probe German defenses along their shared border, and the British Expeditionary Force was just beginning to assemble in France to meet the German threat when Polish resistance collapsed. This tentative period in the West, called the "Phoney War," continued through the winter of 1939–1940 while conflict erupted in the East between Russia and defiant Finland.

THE WINTER WAR

Known as the Red Tsar, Joseph Stalin was as much an imperialist as a communist, and he exploited his secret protocol with Hitler to rein in countries bordering Russia that had broken free after the last tsar, Nicholas II, abdicated in 1917. Having weakened the Red Army by purging thousands of its senior officers, Stalin used threats

The map shows the Red Army's invasion routes (red) early in the Winter War in late 1939 and the opposing paths of Finnish defenders (blue), who rebuffed Soviet troops. Despite Russia's advantage in manpower and weapons, the Finns were better prepared to fight on their own rugged ground in snow and bitter cold. The Soviets would not break through the Mannerheim Line until February 1940.

against neighboring countries before resorting to armed force. In October 1939, he pressured Latvia, Estonia, and Lithuania into accepting Soviet military bases, which soon enabled Russia to reabsorb those Baltic states without waging war. Stalin then targeted Finland, insisting that it accept a Soviet naval base and cede territory between the Baltic Sea and Lake Ladoga to provide a buffer zone for Leningrad. Finnish leaders in Helsinki refused.

On November 30, 1939, the Red Army invaded Finland, committing over 600,000 troops against fewer than 200,000 defenders. The Soviets were confounded by agile Finnish soldiers, many on skis, who knew the terrain far better than their bewildered foes. As one Russian soldier recalled, "There were no roads, no settlements—just forests and lakes. Nothing to get your bearings from." Disoriented and poorly commanded, the invaders took heavy losses. They performed "like a badly led orchestra," remarked the Finnish chief, Field Marshal Carl Gustaf Mannerheim, who counterattacked in December and pushed the Soviets back from his Mannerheim Line above Leningrad. Although the Russians bombed Helsinki and other targets and had a huge advantage in manpower and armor, the Finns waylaid Russian tanks and were better prepared to fight on rugged ground in snow and bitter cold. Not until Stalin dispatched more troops in January 1940 under Gen. Semyon Timoshenko did the Russians gain a foothold. Timoshenko launched repeated attacks against the Mannerheim Line and broke through in February 1940, prompting Finland to finally yield on March 13. Timoshenko's heavy reinforcements overwhelmed Finnish defenders, one of whom was to ruefully later reflect: "There were more Russians than we had bullets." The Finns were forced to cede substantial territory.

The Red Army's poor showing in the Winter War reinforced Hitler's conviction that when the time came, his forces would crush the Soviets. But he overlooked another lesson of the conflict—Stalin's capacity to recover from setbacks by drawing on deep reserves of Russian manpower. ■

BELOW: **The Finns waged the Winter War with ski troops often outmaneuvering and outfighting the Soviet invaders.**

WAR IN THE WEST

++++++++++++

Hitler was surprised when Britain and France, after yielding to him at Munich, responded to the invasion of Poland by declaring war, but he was not dismayed. He looked forward to ending the Reich's long-standing dispute with France, which had regained the border province of Alsace-Lorraine from Germany under the Treaty of Versailles, by defeating the French once and for all. And he hoped that the British, whose Anglo-Saxon heritage and imperial prowess he admired, would then come to terms and accept German domination of continental Europe. While his generals planned a blitzkrieg that would slash through the Low Countries to Paris, Hitler decided to precede that offensive by invading neutral Norway and establishing naval bases there. That would secure the Reich's northern flank against Allied intervention in Norway, which Hitler anticipated, and protect vital shipments of Swedish iron ore to Germany from the Norwegian port of Narvik. Neutral Denmark would also be invaded, leaving Sweden little choice but to accommodate Germany if it hoped to preserve its own neutrality.

On April 9, German air, naval, and ground assaults overwhelmed Denmark, which fell within hours. Oslo and other Norwegian ports were then captured by troops delivered by sea, but these naval operations proved costly. Britain's Royal Navy and Norwegian coastal batteries sank 15 troop transports, and the German fleet lost roughly half its warships.

Allied forces—British troops, French Foreign Legionnaires, and exiled Polish soldiers—landed in April

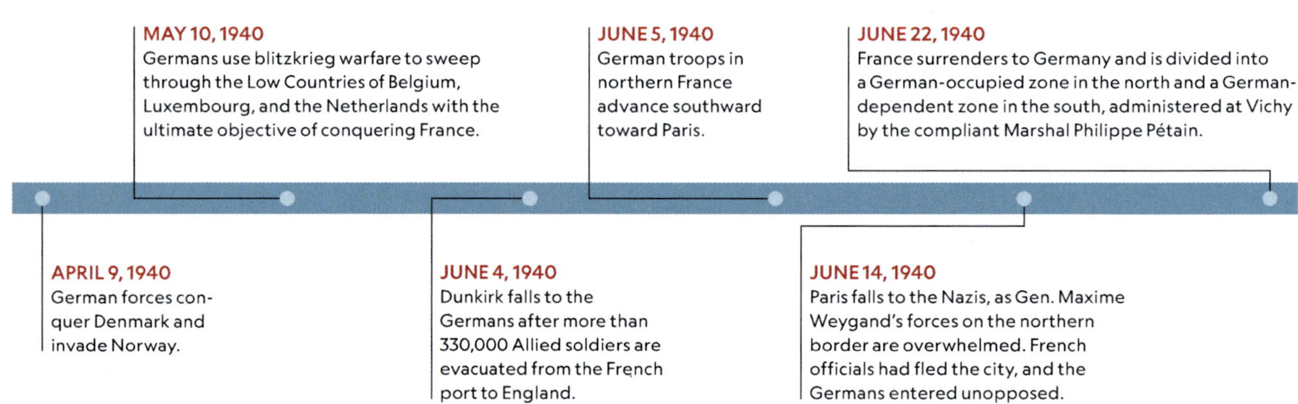

and fought alongside Norwegians, reclaiming Narvik in May. By then, however, the Germans had invaded France, and Allied commanders withdrew forces for more pressing engagements. The Norwegians capitulated in June.

BREAKING THE MAGINOT LINE

The long-anticipated German offensive on France that began on May 10, 1940, still surprised the Allies. British intelligence officers estimated that as many as 124 German divisions were positioned in western Germany by May 3. The bulk of these were poised near the German borders with Belgium, Luxembourg, and the Netherlands. Allied commanders expected their foes to skirt Germany's border with France, where the French Maginot Line was strongest, and instead descend on Paris through Belgium.

The German plan of attack, involving three army groups, was shrewdly designed to exploit the expected Allied defense of neutral Belgium. Army Group C, led by Gen. Wilhelm Ritter von Leeb, remained opposite the Maginot Line along the French border to keep defenders tied down. General Bock's Army Group B invaded Holland and northern Belgium on May 10, drawing three French armies and the British Expeditionary Force

RIGHT: **French troops stranded in Belgium were captured by panzers of Army Group A as the Germans swept across northern France toward the sea.**

German notations in red on a map of northern France show Gen. Heinz Wilhelm Guderian's XIX Panzer Corps advancing to the Somme River estuary by May 20 and Gen. Georg Hans Reinhardt's XLI Panzer Corps (designated XXXXI) advancing on a parallel path to the north. At center is Gen. Erwin Rommel's Seventh Panzer Division (7 Pz) of XV Panzer Corps near Arras. His forces pursued the retreating French Ninth Army. By late May, the only hope for beleaguered Allied forces was to fall back to the port of Dunkirk, from which they might be evacuated to England (see sidebar p. 18).

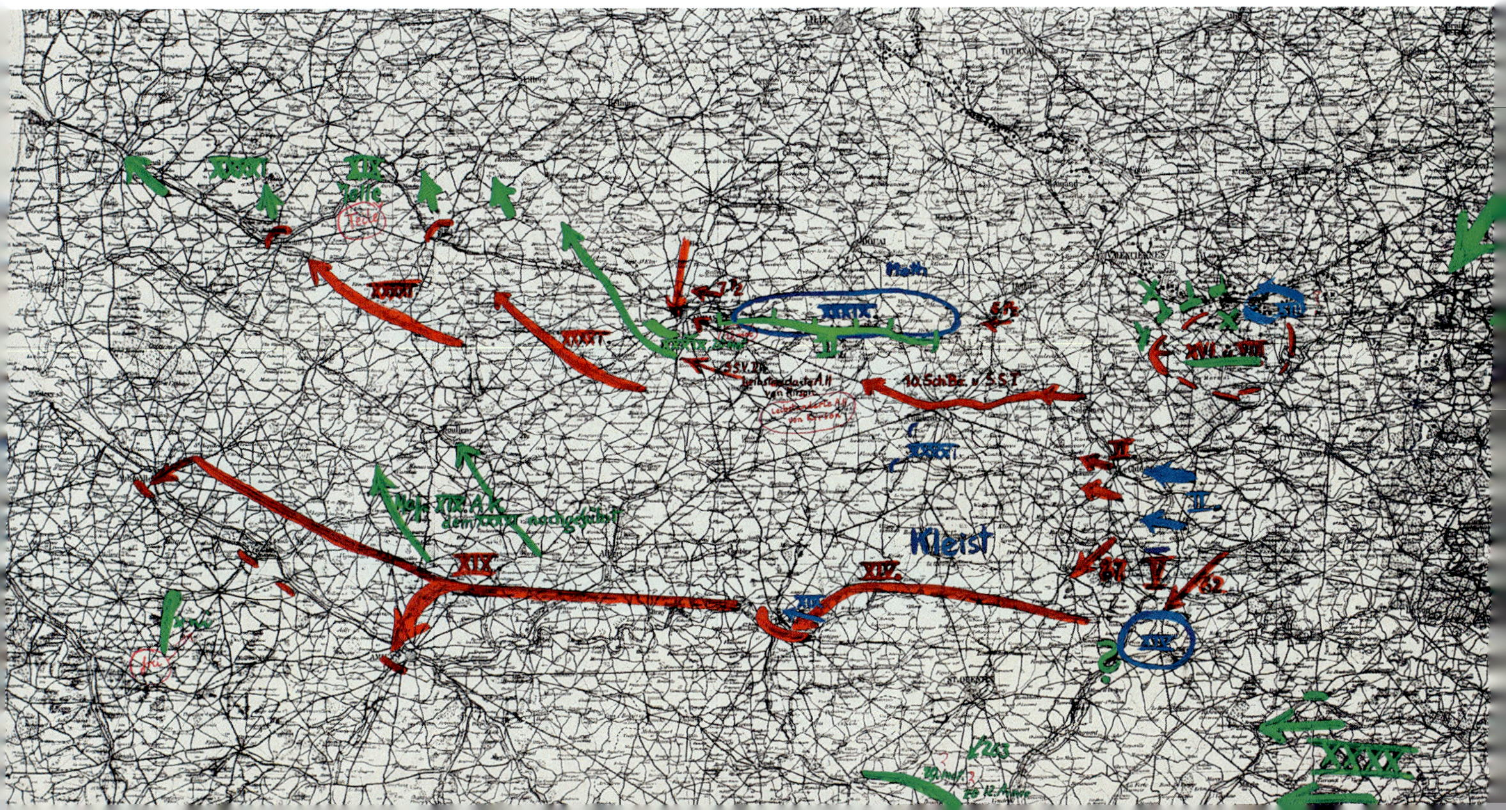

northward. Those troops were soon trapped, sprung by panzers (armored units) at the forefront of General Rundstedt's Army Group A that advanced through the Ardennes—a forest extending from Luxembourg into southern Belgium that was mistakenly considered impassable by tanks. A German officer feared his tanks would be detected as they churned through the Ardennes, but he did not spot "a single French reconnaissance aircraft."

By May 14, the panzers crossed into northern France and smashed enemy lines around Sedan with help from the Luftwaffe's Stukas. Armored corps were soon pouring through breaches in the Maginot Line along the French border with Belgium and racing toward the sea, a thrust that would cut off nearly a million Allied troops to the north. As one German officer boasted, "The rapid movements and flexible handling of our panzers bewildered the enemy."

THE FALL OF FRANCE

General Maxime Weygand, the 73-year-old commander charged with defending France in June 1940, had helped halt the German advance on Paris in 1914. But now huge losses left him with barely 70 divisions to face nearly 130 German divisions. Blistering attacks by panzers and the Luftwaffe had woefully reduced his armored and air forces. Short of resources, Weygand settled on a "checkerboard" defense in which open

DELIVERANCE AT DUNKIRK

When evacuations from Dunkirk began on May 26, 1940, British commanders figured that only 45,000 of the nearly 400,000 Allied troops there could be rescued before Germans captured the port. Marshy ground and mechanical breakdowns slowed the panzer tanks, but infantry assaults overwhelmed Belgian troops defending the port. On May 28, Belgium surrendered. By then, German warplanes had blasted Dunkirk's docks and strafed soldiers on the beach, a task that one pilot called "unadulterated killing." Cloudy skies and dense smoke over Dunkirk often obscured targets, however, and British fighter pilot attacks on German bombers helped protect the evacuations.

Heroic rearguard actions by French troops enabled a motley fleet of some 1,000 vessels, ranging from tugboats to Royal Navy destroyers, to extract 338,000 Allied soldiers before Dunkirk fell on June 4. The rescue of nearly 225,000 British Expeditionary Force troops encouraged the British to keep fighting the war. More than 100,000 French soldiers were saved too, but France had lost roughly a third of its forces since May 10.

As the last evacuees returned from Dunkirk, Britain's new prime minister, Winston Churchill, warned the public, "Wars are not won by evacuations."

Soldiers wade to a ship sent to evacuate them from Dunkirk. Some 338,000 Allied troops were rescued.

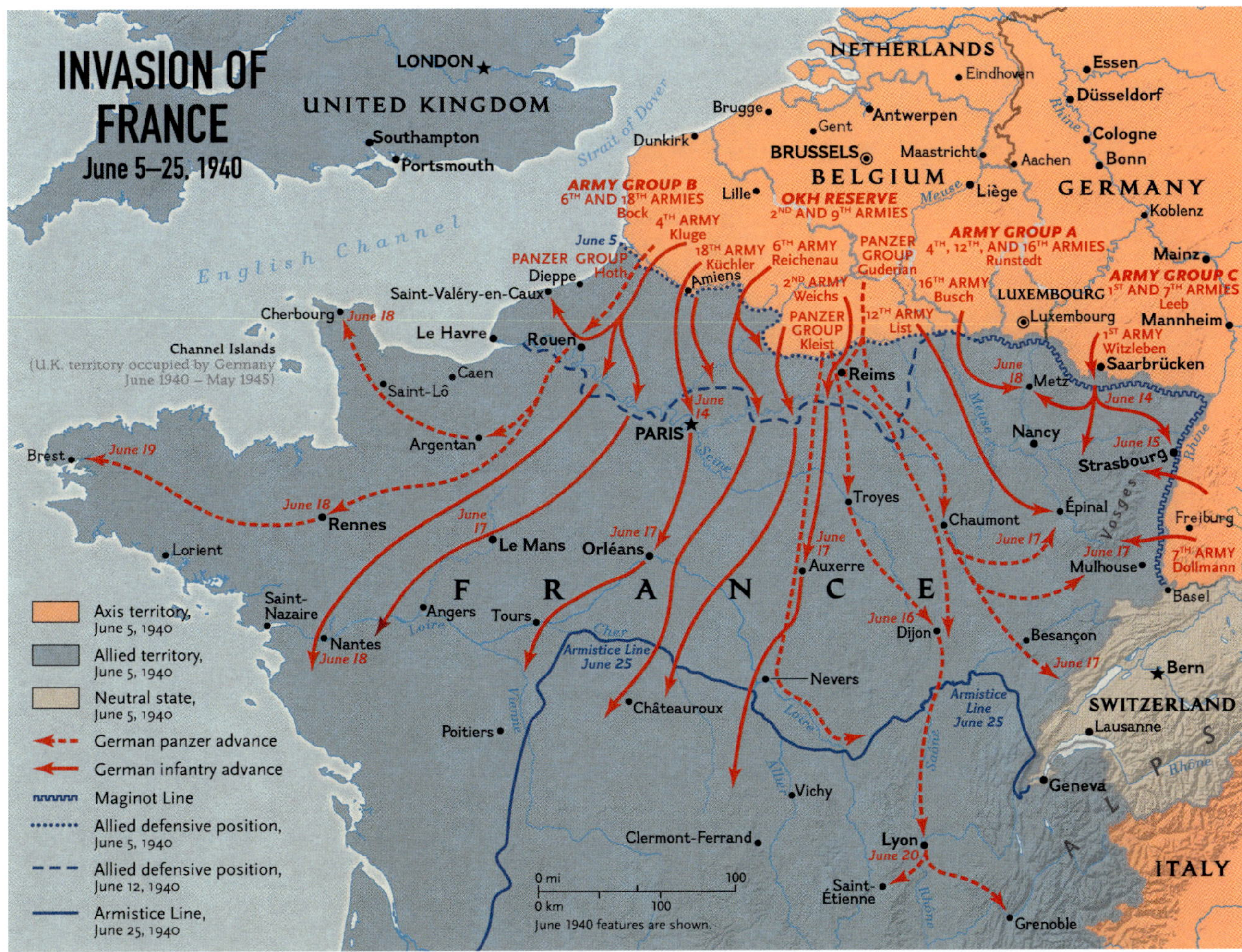

Panzers under Generals Hoth, Kleist, and Guderian (dashed red lines) and infantry of Army Groups A and B and the OKH (Army High Command) Reserve (solid red lines) advanced from a front on June 5 along the Somme and Aisne Rivers in northern France (dotted blue line) to a front on June 12 (dashed blue line) that lay near Paris, which fell two days later. Army Group C then pierced the Maginot Line along the French border with Germany. When the armistice to which France yielded on June 22 took effect three days later, a boundary was drawn between the German-occupied and Vichy zones (solid blue line).

spaces alternated with clusters of troops in villages or woods. He ordered them to cling to those positions, adding that officers "must be filled with the grim desire to stand and fight to the death."

No amount of French determination, however, could thwart the Germans. Army Group B, aligned west along the Somme River, opened hostilities on June 5. Seasoned armored units transferred from Group A, including Rommel's Seventh Panzer Division. These blasted French defenders, then swept around them and forged ahead. "All quiet forward," Rommel reported, "enemy in shreds." On June 8, his panzers reached the Seine River west of Paris. A day later, Army Group A joined the attack and crossed the Aisne River, bolstered by two panzer corps under General Heinz Wilhelm Guderian; these reached the Marne River east of Paris on the 13th. By then, French officials had fled the capital and the Germans entered unopposed on June 14.

Marshal Philippe Pétain agreed to an armistice that divided France into a German-occupied zone in the north and west and a Vichy zone in the south administered for the occupiers by the compliant Pétain. Hitler accepted the surrender of French forces on June 22 in the same railway carriage outside Paris where German generals had yielded to the Allies in 1918. ■

BATTLE FOR BRITAIN

+++++++++++++

On May 13, 1940, Winston Churchill vowed to vanquish Germany while promising the public nothing in the interim "but blood, toil, tears and sweat." He pledged that Britain would stand tall "against a monstrous tyranny, never surpassed in the dark, lamentable catalogue of human crime." Hitler envisioned a land invasion of England, starting with an all-out assault by the Luftwaffe on the Royal Air Force (RAF). The Luftwaffe launched attacks in July on English ports and convoys that proved very costly. Luftwaffe bombers proved vulnerable to swift, maneuverable Supermarine Spitfires and Hawker Hurricanes.

On August 1, Hitler ordered the Luftwaffe to overpower the RAF "with all the forces at its command and in the shortest possible time." British fighter bases and aircraft factories were targeted by German bombers escorted mainly by powerful Me-109s, whose pilots would engage in lethal dogfights against British aircraft. The Battle of Britain between the Luftwaffe and the RAF would determine whether Churchill's island nation could prevail or might soon be overrun.

DOGFIGHTS FOR HIGH STAKES

Elevated by Hitler from the rank of field marshal in July 1940, Reich Marshal Hermann Göring believed that his Luftwaffe alone could defeat the British, precluding the planned invasion of England, dubbed Operation Sea Lion. Göring was an erratic, insecure figure addicted to

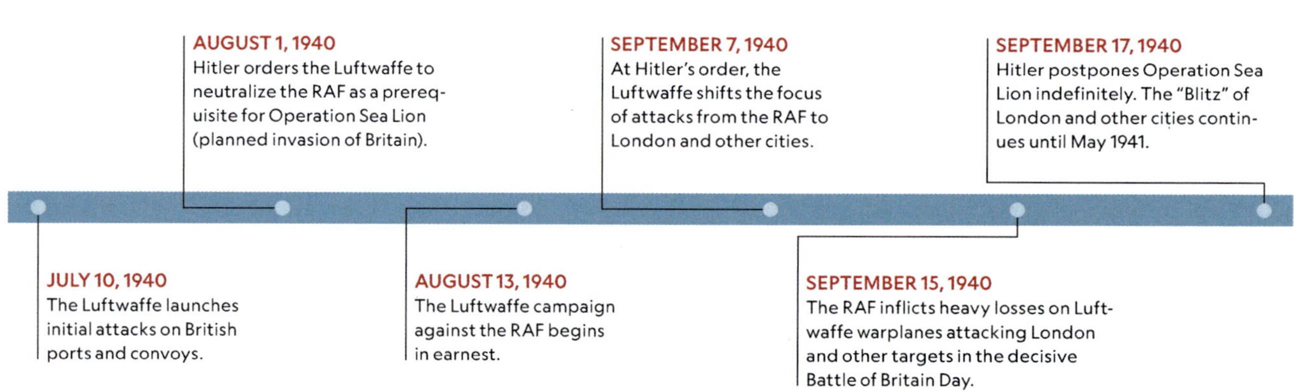

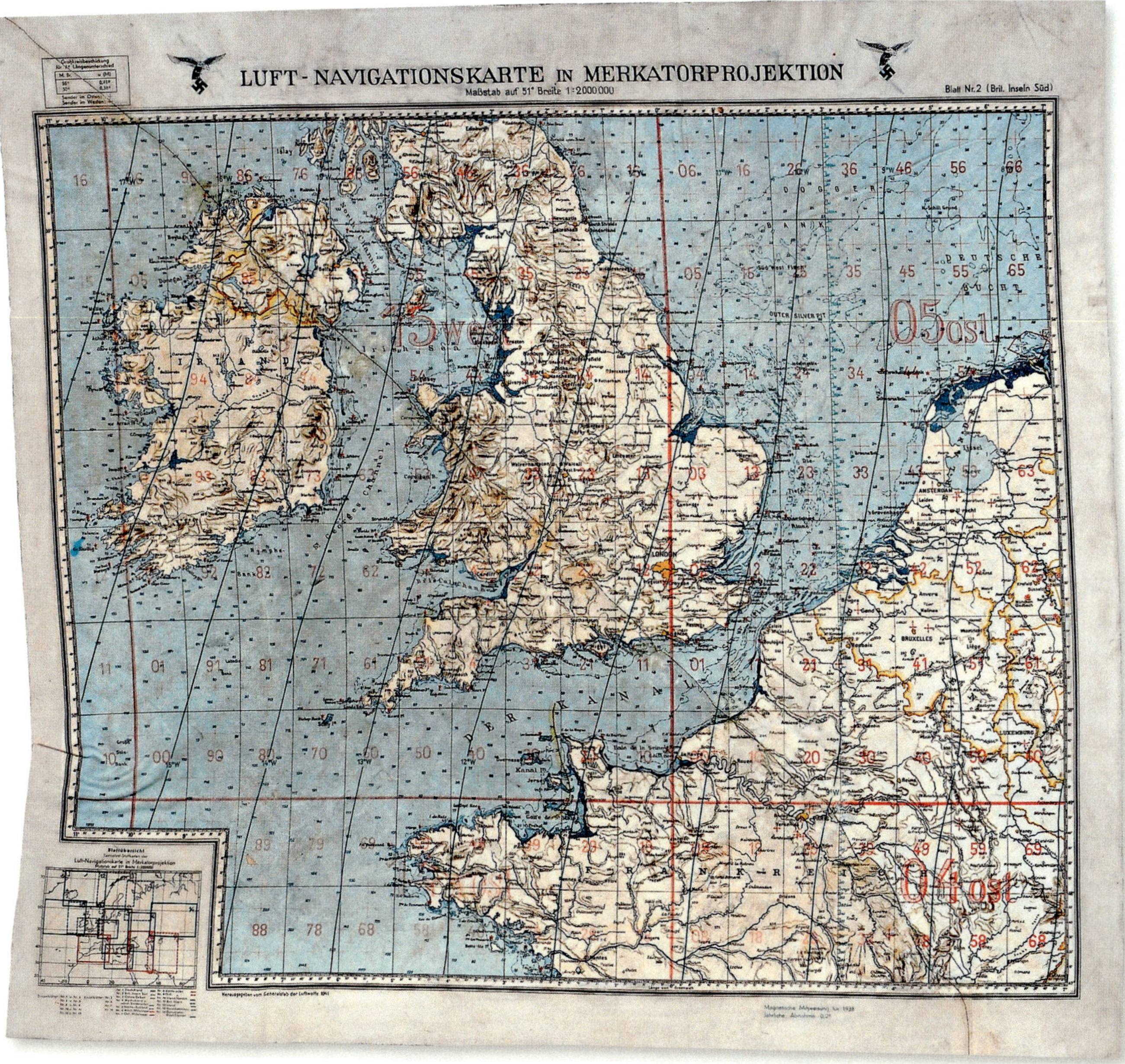

This Luftwaffe map for the Battle of Britain was printed on cloth so airmen could easily carry it and conceal it if they were captured. It combines a rectilinear Mercator projection with lines representing Earth's curvature.

morphine, which he began taking after he was shot during Hitler's abortive Munich Putsch in 1923. Anxious to impress Hitler after the Luftwaffe's failure at Dunkirk, he launched massive attacks against the RAF in mid-August. But in the ensuing dogfights, the British often downed more German aircraft than they lost, aided by radar and the agility of Spitfires and Hurricanes. The formidable German Me-109s were often short of fuel by the time they engaged the enemy. Göring ordered all bombing missions closely escorted by fighters, which kept pilots from pouncing on RAF warplanes. It was hard to win dogfights, one German ace complained, when you put the "dog on a chain."

Yet the sheer weight of the Luftwaffe offensive wore down RAF Fighter Command. By late August, many of its bases were damaged and it was short of pilots. Britain's large complement of foreign fighter pilots probably saved the day, including 145 from Poland and many from New Zealand and Canada. In September, Hitler gave Fighter Command a reprieve when he shifted attacks away from RAF bases to London, in retaliation for the British bombing of Berlin. Göring miscalculated that the city would be lightly defended. On September 15, Fighter Command—which had used the respite to repair airfields and rush newly trained pilots into action—downed nearly 60 incoming warplanes. Two days later, Hitler postponed Operation Sea Lion.

A PUNISHING BLITZ

German plans to invade Britain with aerial blitzkrieg were thwarted, but the Blitz was just beginning. Punishing German air raids on London and other cities continued into the spring of 1941, mostly conducted at night, when RAF fighters and antiaircraft batteries were less effective. Darkness also made it harder for bombers to hit prime targets such as power stations that were designated on Luftwaffe maps. German efforts to guide pilots to targets at night using radio beams were countered when the British jammed those signals, but all bombing wreaked havoc on civilians. Children were evacuated to the countryside, and thousands of people slept in the London Underground.

Luftwaffe fire-bombings consumed large parts of London and other cities. By May 1941, the Blitz had killed over 40,000 people and injured many more. Yet the pounding did little to demoralize civilians or fulfill Hitler's principal strategic objective—to eliminate Britain "as a base from which the war against Germany can be continued."

ABOVE: **RAF pilots-in-training wearing parachute packs scramble to their fighters. Britain was guarded by a coastal network of radar stations and observers positioned to alert the RAF and intercept Luftwaffe squadrons before they reached their targets.** BELOW: **Twin-engine Vickers Wellington medium bombers were involved in some of the earliest RAF raids against Germany.**

STRATEGIC BOMBING OF GERMANY

RAF fighters were among the world's best in 1940, but its bombers could not carry large enough payloads to really damage German targets. Early British bombing raids were often retaliatory and their impact more psychological than strategic. Nuisance raids on Berlin in August 1940 enraged Hitler, who vowed that if the British targeted "our cities, then we will raze their cities to the ground." The ensuing Blitz was terrifying for civilians.

To boost British morale and goad Hitler, the RAF bombed Munich on the night of November 8, 1940, while the Führer was addressing so-called Old Fighters of the Nazi Party on the anniversary of his Munich Putsch. The Luftwaffe retaliated by fire-bombing Coventry on November 14, gutting the city center and leaving more than 1,000 people dead or wounded.

The RAF began amassing a force of heavy bombers, many of them four-engine aircraft. Technological advances in guiding aircraft at night and targeted bombing increased the accuracy of those heavy hitters, but their main task was to saturate industrial areas and population centers with blockbuster bombs and incendiaries, far surpassing the destruction wrought by the Luftwaffe. In Churchill's opinion, the only thing that could bring down Hitler was "an absolutely devastating exterminating attack by very heavy bombers from this country upon the Nazi homeland." ■

OPERATION SEA LION

Hitler's order in September 1940 postponing Operation Sea Lion came as a relief for his commanders assigned to carry out the proposed invasion of Britain. German Navy chief Grand Adm. Erich Raeder had nixed an Army plan to land some 30 divisions totaling more than 500,000 troops along a 200-mile (320 km) front on England's south coast. At Raeder's urging, the landing zone was narrowed to about 35 miles (56 km) along the Strait of Dover, where nine German divisions would land, followed by two more waves of troops. That gave Raeder some chance of preventing the Royal Navy from shredding an invasion fleet as it crossed to England. But German Army chief of staff Gen. Franz Halder worried that invading on a narrow front would allow the British Army to focus its forces. "I might just as well put the troops straight through a sausage machine!" he warned.

This narrow option exacerbated another snag faced by the Navy, which possessed no landing craft and had to hastily assemble and convert more than 1,000 river barges. Meanwhile, the Army rushed to convert tanks so that they could be unloaded in the water and drive onto British shores. By late August, 200 tanks had been converted into watertight submersibles with air-intake tubes that could operate at depths up to 15 feet (4.5 m). Tank crews could see above water through periscopes but could not spot obstructions placed underwater off beaches.

Raeder, Halder, and other commanders feared Operation Sea Lion might falter even if the Luftwaffe succeeded in neutralizing the RAF. Though the Blitz continued, the British public took great heart in defying German bombardment and invasion. Churchill vowed that the enemy would be driven back into the sea and devoured: "We are waiting for the long-promised invasion," he declared. "So are the fishes."

British home guards train to defend their homeland against a German invasion.

OPERATION BARBAROSSA

+++++++++++++

Beginning at dawn on June 22, 1941, more than three million German troops invaded Soviet territory, including the recently annexed Baltic states, eastern Poland, and Bessarabia, where troops from neighboring Romania and other Axis countries joined the offensive. By dismissing warnings of that massive attack, Stalin left his forces woefully vulnerable. On the first day, the Luftwaffe destroyed over 1,200 Russian aircraft, many of them on the ground. Within a week, the invaders were pouring through yawning gaps in the Stalin Line along the prewar Soviet border and taking prisoners in droves.

Like previous campaigns, Operation Barbarossa (see map opposite) was planned as a blitzkrieg led by armored units. While Field Marshal Leeb's Army Group North targeted Leningrad and Field Marshal Rundstedt's Army Group South invaded southern Ukraine, Field Marshal Bock's Army Group Center pressed toward Moscow—an advance spearheaded by General Guderian's Second Panzer Group and Gen. Hermann Hoth's Third Panzer Group, which converged at Minsk in late June and cut off a half million enemy troops. In July, panzers enveloped Smolensk, within 200 miles (320 km)

> WE HAVE UNDERESTIMATED THE RUSSIAN COLOSSUS.
>
> —FRANZ HALDER, GERMAN ARMY CHIEF OF STAFF

LEFT: **In 1941, six million Soviet troops were killed or captured by German invaders like these motorized infantrymen—panzer grenadiers clearing out Russian sharpshooters near Smolensk.**

German forces advanced boldly through early December 1941, when Russian troops around Moscow counterattacked. In 1941 alone, German invaders killed or captured six million Soviet troops. The Red Army endured such losses by enlisting 34 million men and women during the war.

of Moscow, but Hitler then halted the advance and ordered Guderian to help Army Group South encircle Kiev. German Army chief of staff Gen. Franz Halder objected and urged Hitler to keep tanks and motorized infantry driving toward Moscow. Privately, Halder feared even that might not bring victory. "We have underestimated the Russian colossus," he wrote. When the Russians lost a dozen divisions, he added, they would "put up another dozen," whereas the Germans were losing more men and vehicles fighting their way across Russia's "endless spaces" than they could readily replace.

In late September, the advance on Moscow resumed, but muddy ground slowed Army Group Center to a crawl while Army Group North laid siege to Leningrad and Army Group South entered the Crimean Peninsula. In late November, panzers churned forward on frozen terrain to within a dozen miles (19 km) of Moscow before stalling in drifting snow and subzero temperatures. Meanwhile, Soviet forces around the capital had been reinforced and were poised to push the invaders back.

SECRET PREPARATIONS TO INVADE RUSSIA

Operation Barbarossa called for German soldiers to invade an immense country about which they knew relatively little. German intelligence compiled reports, guides, maps, and atlases for officers who might soon be targeting major cities like Moscow and Leningrad or vital regions like Ukraine, Russia's fertile "breadbasket," which had ports on the Black Sea. Some of that guidance came from published sources, which were not always reliable. Highways shown on Russian maps, for example, might turn out to be dirt paths. Stalin's regime concealed information about strategic port facilities, industrial areas, and transportation networks. To help chart likely targets for the invasion, the Luftwaffe conducted high-altitude photoreconnaissance missions over Russia.

Many of the atlases and reports prepared for Operation Barbarossa contained photographs from ground level, ranging from a panoramic view of a huge Soviet military parade in Leningrad Square to pictures of forlorn Russian towns. Despite ample evidence that the Soviet Union was industrializing, Hitler viewed the nation as hopelessly backward and planned to cleanse fertile areas like Ukraine of Russian peasants to make room for German colonists, whom he envisioned living in "handsome villages connected by the best roads."

Atlases and guides were distributed to trusted commanders, but preparations for Operation Barbarossa involved so many officials that secrecy was compromised. Germans who spied for the Soviets—such as Richard Sorge, a journalist who learned of the invasion from the German ambassador in Tokyo—warned Moscow of the forthcoming attack. Stalin dismissed those reports as Allied fabrications meant to prod him into war against Hitler. When Soviet generals suggested a preemptive strike in May 1941, Stalin warned: "If you're going to provoke the Germans . . . heads will roll."

Intelligence for Operation Barbarossa even included reconnaissance of remote towns invaders may encounter.

THE BATTLE FOR MOSCOW

Staggered by the swift German advances, Stalin ordered Russian soldiers who retreated without authorization to be shot. Gen. Georgi Zhukov was ousted as the Red Army's chief of general staff after protesting Stalin's refusal to withdraw beleaguered troops from Kiev. Stalin then relented and summoned Zhukov to defend Moscow. As Russians commemorated the Bolshevik Revolution in Red Square on November 7, Stalin blasted the enemy. "If they want a war of extermination, they shall have it," he declared. Heavy reinforcements arrived from Siberia, summoned when spy Richard Sorge reported from Tokyo that Japan would not invade the Soviet Far East.

The Soviet counterattack began north of Moscow on December 5. Zhukov's forces pushed west from the capital and troops led by Gen. Semyon Timoshenko advanced to the south. Ski troops and Siberian cavalry breached German lines, and Russian crews attacked in tanks that started promptly in deep freezes while their foes were forced to light fires under vehicles to get them going. Many German troops suffered severe frostbite. Lack of winter clothing forced some to take coats and scarves from Russians. One Soviet officer remarked that Germans who had seemed so strong in the summer were now "miserable, crooked, snotty guys wrapped in woolen kerchiefs stolen from old women in villages."

On December 16, Hitler ordered forces reeling under

the Russian onslaught to stand fast. Some commanders refused to comply and were relieved by Hitler, including Gen. Erich Hoepner, who did not share the Führer's belief that sheer willpower could overcome this crisis. "The will is there," Hoepner stated. "The strength is lacking."

CARNAGE IN THE "MEAT-GRINDER"

Stalin ordered the Red Army to encircle and destroy the German Army Group Center west of Moscow. General Zhukov intended to close the trap at Vyazma, nearly 120 miles (190 km) from Moscow, but the German Ninth Army and other units clung to a salient between Vyazma and Rzhev that resembled a peninsula, against which waves of Soviet troops crashed. Hitler placed the Ninth Army under a new commander, Gen. Walther Model. When Hitler opposed Model's plan to send a panzer corps to reinforce Rzhev, the general posed a question that few German officers would have dared ask: "Who commands the Ninth Army, my Führer, you or I?"

> IF THEY WANT A WAR OF EXTERMINATION, THEY SHALL HAVE IT.
>
> —JOSEPH STALIN, SUPREME LEADER OF THE U.S.S.R.

Model prevailed and held the salient against fierce attacks by Soviet tanks and troops, who suffered such heavy losses around Rzhev that they dubbed it the "meat-grinder."

Come spring, Rzhev remained under German control; the German line held west of Moscow. They now faced a drawn-out conflict that worried German officers with long memories. The Rzhev area came to resemble the dreaded battlefields of World War I, drenched in the blood of both sides time and again until the losers were bled dry. ■

Dated August 4, 1941, this Russian map shows Moscow divided into five defensive sectors with outer and inner rings of barricades, tank traps, and gun emplacements.

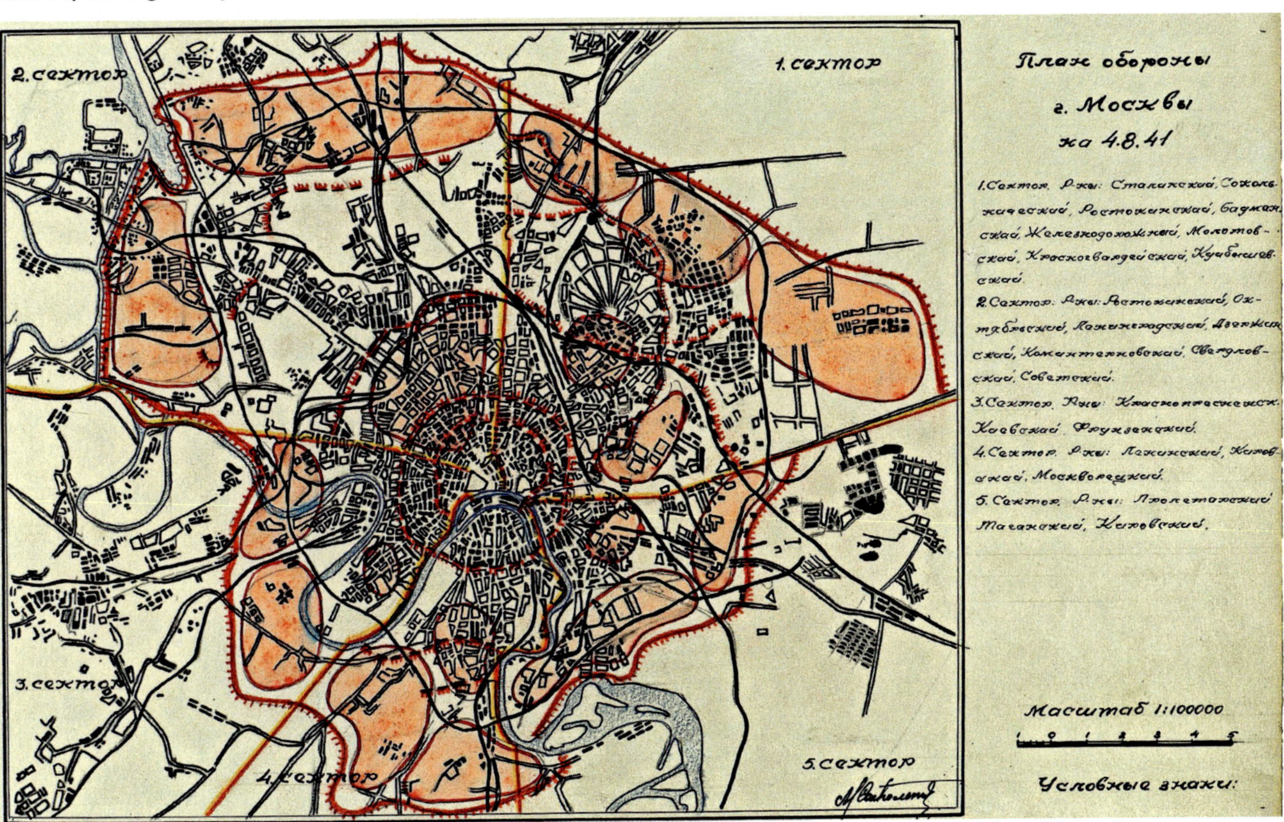

Shown here dressed in court regalia at his enthronement ceremony in 1926, Emperor Hirohito held the throne of Japan by divine right and served as commander in chief of the armed forces.

CHAPTER 2

WAR IN THE PACIFIC

PRELUDE TO WAR–1943

Japan pursued expansionist policies throughout the early 20th century, and Japanese leaders resented U.S. efforts to deter them from subjugating China and seizing vulnerable European colonies such as French Indochina, British-ruled Burma and Malaya, and the oil-rich Dutch East Indies. Hadn't these same Americans colonized Hawaii and taken the Philippines from Spain, they asked. Following Japan's invasion of China in 1937, foreign minister Yosuke Matsuoka took the tactical decision to join the Tripartite Pact with Axis powers Germany and Italy in October 1940, aiming to make the U.S. more cautious and willing to compromise. President Franklin D. Roosevelt believed that the appeasement of Hitler at Munich proved that yielding to an aggressor was perilous and that only firm opposition to the occupation might change Japanese minds. However, if the price for peace was to kowtow to America and withdraw from China, then Japan was resolved to fight, and its targets would include the U.S. Pacific Fleet in Hawaii.

Adm. Isoroku Yamamoto, commander of Japan's Combined Fleet, hoped to smash the U.S. Pacific Fleet with warplanes before the American war effort geared up. The surprise attack on Pearl Harbor in December 1941 marked the start of a Japanese offensive that stretched from Hawaii to Burma. The battered U.S. Pacific Fleet revived under Adm. Chester Nimitz, whose forces prevailed at the Battle of Midway in June 1942. Ensuing battles saw American and British Commonwealth troops defeat Japanese forces on Guadalcanal, Papua, and New Guinea. By April 1943, when U.S. fighter pilots shot down Yamamoto, Japan was in trouble, fighting an American colossus that was bringing its full weight to bear.

1914–1918
Clashes between Japanese and Chinese troops in Peking (Beijing) lead to a full-scale invasion of China.

DECEMBER 13, 1937
Japanese troops take Nanking (Nanjing), the Chinese Nationalist capital, and commit massive atrocities.

SEPTEMBER 27, 1940
Japan joins the Axis alliance, signing the Tripartite Pact with Germany and Italy.

DECEMBER 7–8, 1941
Japanese offensive begins with attacks on U.S. and British territories in the Pacific.

FEBRUARY 27, 1942
Japanese forces win the Battle of the Java Sea.

MARCH 11, 1942
Gen. Douglas MacArthur is ordered to evacuate from the Philippines to Australia, where he will take command of Allied forces in the Pacific.

JUNE 4–7, 1942
U.S. Pacific Fleet wins the pivotal Battle of Midway.

NOVEMBER 13–15, 1942
U.S. Navy forces win the Naval Battle of Guadalcanal.

APRIL 18, 1943
Admiral Yamamoto is killed when U.S. fighter pilots down his plane off Bougainville.

ASCENT OF THE AXIS ALLIANCE

+++++++++++++

When 24-year-old Hirohito became emperor of Japan on December 25, 1926, his reign was designated *Showa,* meaning "illustrious peace." Soon, however, Japan became mired in conflicts, which Hirohito oversaw as commander in chief. Hirohito's commanders gained clout as Japan became a modern military power and gained territory overseas, including Taiwan and Korea—acquired from China. The Great Depression increased pressure for Japan to enlarge its armed forces, expand its empire, and acquire raw materials and captive markets overseas.

In September 1931, officers of the Kwantung Army, assigned to protect Japanese residents in Manchuria, staged an incident to start a conflict. Hirohito remained passive as Japanese commanders in Korea sent more troops into Manchuria. When Japan prevailed, Hirohito commended the officers for acting in "self-defense," signaling tacit permission for further military adventurism. Japan invaded Shanghai in 1932, and withdrew from the League of Nations in 1933.

THE INVASION OF CHINA

In July 1937, Chinese soldiers clashed with Japanese forces at the Marco Polo Bridge in Peking. Emperor Hirohito authorized an invasion to "chastise the Chinese Army." Japanese soldiers soon secured Peking, but the conflict escalated. In August, Chinese Nationalist leader Chiang Kai-shek drew the invaders into a punishing battle for Shanghai. Japanese troops took Shanghai and proceeded to devastate Nanking, the Nationalist capital. Taking no prisoners, they went from shooting soldiers to targeting civilians. Thousands of women were raped, and at least 200,000 people were killed.

The "Rape of Nanking" turned U.S. public opinion against Japan. Meanwhile, Mao Zedong's Chinese Communists waged guerrilla warfare against the invaders. The conflict dragged on and left Japan facing a crucial decision—whether to pull back, as the U.S. urged, or expand its offensive to include Indochina and other European colonies in the Far East. ■

ABOVE: **Japanese troops cheer in Shanghai in 1937.**

IMPERIAL RIVALRY IN THE FAR EAST

In the 17th century, European trading companies cleared the way for the Netherlands to acquire the Dutch East Indies and Britain to colonize India, Burma, and Malaya. By the late 1800s, France ruled most of Indochina, and China was subject to a debilitating opium trade, enforced by Britain. U.S. forces occupied the Philippines during the Spanish-American War in 1898.

Japan vowed to unite the region under Asian rule, supplanting all Western colonizers. Starting around 1870, cartographers copied foreign maps to chart a path of imperial expansion into *gaihozu*, or "outer lands." Japanese surveyors disguised as traveling merchants made vital military maps of China. Tokyo strategically targeted European colonies, which became vulnerable in 1940 as Germany overran Holland, defeated France, and menaced Britain. Swift conquests would provide labor and fuel for its imperial war effort. "Seize this golden opportunity!" urged Army Minister Shunroku Hata.

Japanese forces did just that in September 1940, crossing into Indochina. Further advances followed into British Malaya and the Dutch East Indies. The Philippines, however, stood in the way. If bypassed, that would leave U.S. forces in the heart of Japan's intended realm. If attacked, that meant war with America.

A Japanese military map of an area near Pyongyang in Korea (now North Korea) shows the reach of the imperialistic ambitions of Japan as it entered into World War II.

JAPAN'S STUNNING OFFENSIVE

+++++++++++++

When Germany invaded Russia in late June 1941, Japanese leaders debated whether to join their Axis ally and attack the Soviets or proceed with plans to target European colonies in the Far East. They did not rule out invading Russia if the German advance on Moscow succeeded, but they saw more to be gained by seizing those Asian colonies and their resources, which they hoped to use to subdue China and sustain a vast empire they called the Greater East Asia Co-Prosperity Sphere. French Indochina and the Dutch East Indies were fairly easy targets, but the British would not yield Malaya and Burma without a fight, and their American allies would have to be dealt with as well. On July 2, Tokyo authorized "preparations for war with Great Britain and the United States."

After Japan took all of Indochina in late July and was subjected to an American oil embargo, Emperor Hirohito asked Prime Minister Hideki Tojo—a general committed to imperial expansion—to make one last diplomatic effort to avert war. Talks in Washington faltered after deciphered cables from Tokyo indicated that Japan would attack if a deal was not reached by November 30. President Roosevelt declined to make concessions under the gun. On December 1, Admiral Yamamoto gave aircraft carriers already en route the go-ahead to bomb Pearl Harbor (see sidebar p. 35)—one of several blows delivered simultaneously in a vast Japanese offensive that expanded the theater of World War II enormously.

ABOVE: **Admiral Yamamoto (pictured front row, center) designed the Pearl Harbor attack to cripple the U.S. Pacific Fleet.**

DOMINATING THE FAR EAST

Unlike the surprise assault on Pearl Harbor, Japanese attacks on European colonies in the Far East were anticipated, but the war in Europe left those outposts short of military resources. The British High Command knew by November 1941 that Japan might soon launch an offensive directed at Singapore on the southern tip of the Malay Peninsula and dispatched a naval force including the battleship H.M.S. *Prince of Wales* and the heavy

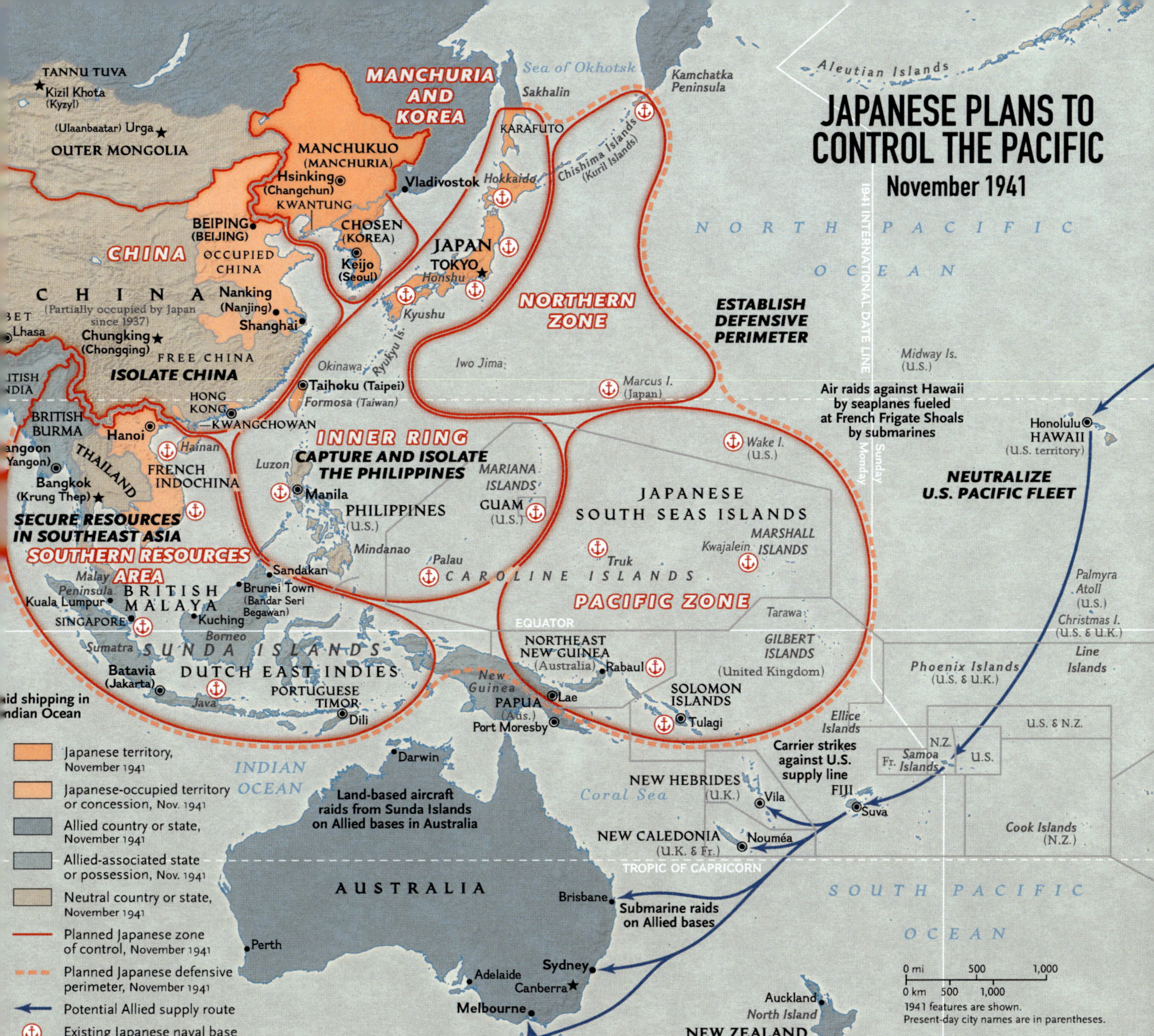

Japan's primary objective was to seize oil, rubber, and other strategic assets in the Southern Resources Area. That meant invading the Dutch East Indies as well as British-ruled Malaya and Burma, which would set Japan at odds with the United States. Anticipating American opposition, Japanese commanders planned to invade the Philippines, within their inner ring of defense, as well as more distant Allied possessions that lay within their defensive perimeter including the Solomon Islands, Hawaii, and even the West Coast of the United States.

cruiser H.M.S. *Repulse,* which arrived in Singapore minus an aircraft carrier that required repairs. Sent out with no fighter cover when the Japanese invasion of Malaya began on December 8, the *Prince of Wales* and *Repulse* were attacked by bombers two days later and went down. To make matters worse, the British commander in Malay, Lt. Gen. Arthur Percival, had almost no tanks to combat those rumbling through the jungle toward Singapore. Percival's troops far outnumbered the Japanese 25th Army, but many of them were demoralized soldiers from India who, when captured, agreed to serve in the Indian National Army, which backed Japan in the hope of freeing India from British rule. On February 15, 1942, after Japanese forces cut off water supplies to bomb-ravaged Singapore, Percival surrendered, capping the worst British defeat of the war.

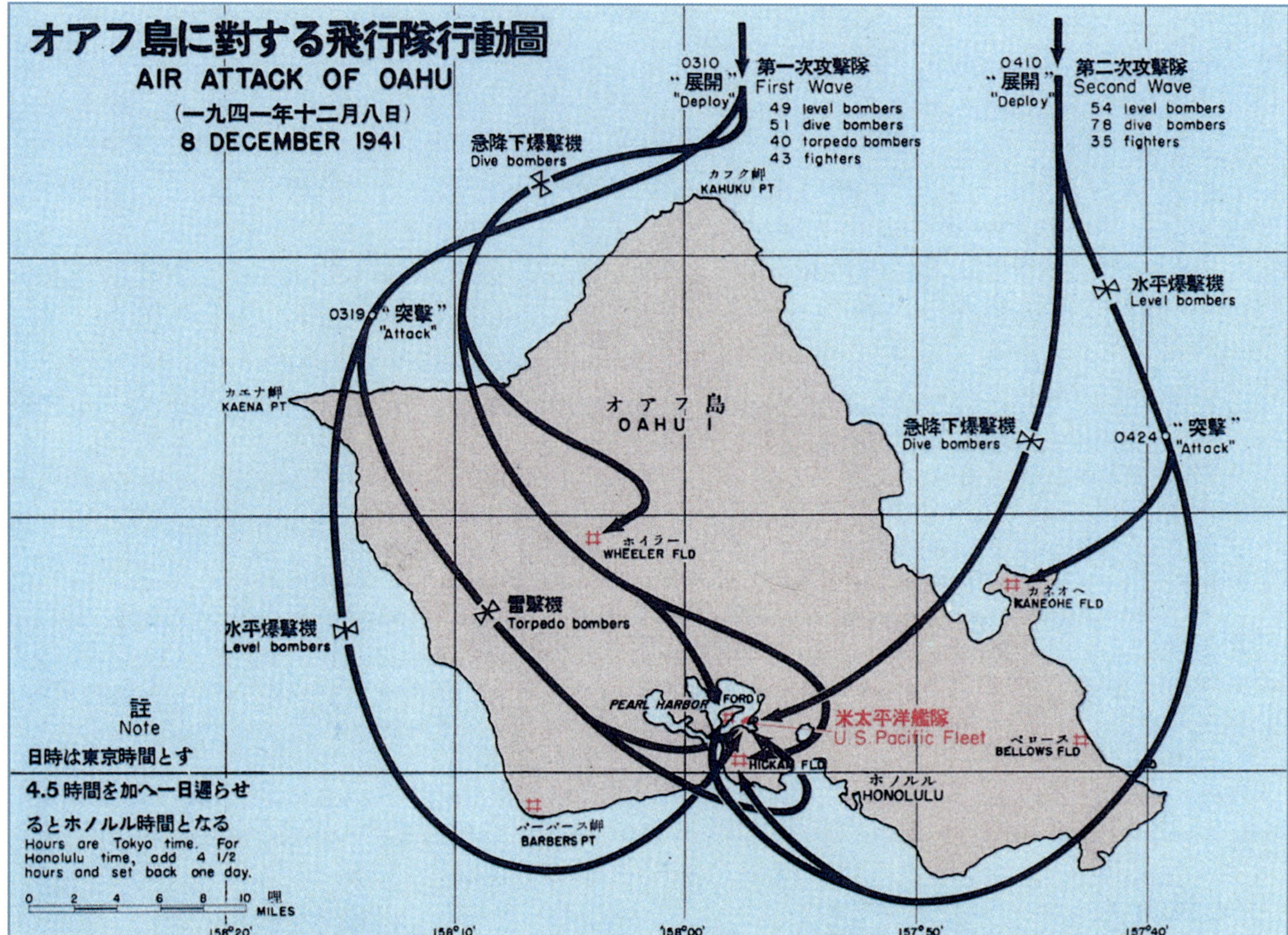

A map derived from a Japanese original using Tokyo time (19 and a half hours later than Hawaii time) delineates the two waves of warplanes that descended on Oahu and Pearl Harbor. The second wave faced alert defenders and lost 20 aircraft, compared with nine losses for the first wave.

By then, much of the Dutch East Indies was occupied by Japanese troops, unopposed by Dutch colonists. After the Netherlands fell to Germany in May 1940, the small Dutch navy under Adm. Karel Doorman was combined with the U.S. Asiatic Fleet and warships of other Allied nations to form a fleet designated ABDA (American, British, Dutch, and Australian), which Doorman led in February against an invasion fleet destined for Java. Defeated in the Battle of the Java Sea, Doorman went down with his ship, and Java fell to Japan on March 12.

> "WE GOT RUN OUT OF BURMA AND IT IS HUMILIATING AS HELL.
>
> —GEN. JOSEPH STILWELL, COMMANDER OF U.S. AND CHINESE FORCES

Around this time, Japanese troops who had invaded Burma captured the capital, Rangoon. They used that port to bring in reinforcements. Overwhelmed, Allied forces consisting of British, Burmese, Indian, and Chinese Nationalist troops—including two divisions led by Lt. Gen. Joseph Stilwell—retreated north to India. Many were killed or captured before the remnant crossed the Indian border to safety in May. Stilwell was in no mood to celebrate. "We got run out of Burma," he said, "and it is humiliating as hell."

THE BATAAN DEATH MARCH

On December 23, 1941, Gen. Douglas MacArthur ordered American and Filipino troops under his command to abandon Manila, the capital of the Philippines, and withdraw to the Bataan Peninsula. Japanese air strikes at Clark Field, northwest of Manila, had destroyed many American warplanes and cleared the way for invasion. By January 1942, 200,000 Japanese troops had besieged 22,000 U.S. soldiers and nearly 60,000 Filipino recruits at Bataan. MacArthur's men fought hard as the invaders forced them back toward their headquarters on the island of Corregidor. Casualties, tropical diseases, and relentless enemy pressure left them in desperate straits.

In March, MacArthur received evacuation orders from President Roosevelt, who did not want to see his star general killed or captured when he could continue to fight for the Pacific out of the Allied base in Australia. MacArthur offered a memorable pledge to those he left behind: "I came through and I shall return." The War Information Office in Washington asked MacArthur's permission to change the "I" to "we" before releasing

ABOVE: **Allied commander Joseph Stilwell retreats from Burma with his men to India.**

ASSAULT ON PEARL HARBOR

By December 7, 1941, U.S. commanders at Pearl Harbor had been warned that hostile action was "possible at any moment," yet they suspected the Japanese would first attack Guam, Wake Island, or Midway, some 1,300 miles (2,100 km) closer to Japan than Oahu. Two aircraft carriers that Yamamoto hoped to attack at Pearl Harbor, U.S.S. *Enterprise* and U.S.S. *Lexington,* had already left to deliver warplanes to Midway and Wake Island. Pearl Harbor was not on high alert.

As shown in the map (at left) retracing the assault in Tokyo time, the first wave of planes approached from the north, ordered to attack by Cmdr. Mitsuo Fuchida at 7:49 a.m. Hawaii time. Their objectives included airfields on Oahu, but their prime targets were the warships moored there. Some bombers came in low and released torpedoes, one of which capsized the battleship U.S.S. *Oklahoma.* A bomb dropped at high level on the battleship U.S.S. *Arizona* penetrated its magazine and detonated a catastrophic explosion. Around 9 a.m., the second wave of warplanes came in. Within a few hours, the attackers sank or badly damaged all eight battleships at Pearl Harbor and 11 other warships, destroyed 170 aircraft, and killed or wounded more than 3,500 Americans. By day's end, the U.S. was committed to war in the Pacific. "Today we are all in the same boat with you," Roosevelt cabled Churchill.

A battle-torn U.S. flag signals devastation but also a day of heroic endurance.

the story to the press. "We shall return" would signal that Americans as a whole were determined to defeat the Japanese and liberate the Philippines. But MacArthur would not allow his statement to be altered. Reclaiming the Philippines was his personal crusade, and he believed that Filipinos had more trust in him than in the U.S. government, which had seemingly abandoned them to the enemy. Stranded on Luzon were some 70,000 American and Filipino troops, whose ordeal grew worse when they were captured.

Unprepared to handle so many prisoners and contemptuous of men who surrendered rather than fight to the death, Japanese soldiers marched their captives nearly 70 miles (112 km) north to a railroad station at San Fernando, where they would be transported to Capas, near Camp O'Donnell, a captured Allied base that would serve as their prison. Already weary and hungry when the march began, they had little to drink and went without food for days. Many who could not keep up and fell were killed by guards or left to die. Those who survived the march were then packed into sweltering boxcars for the trip to Capas. "Some collapsed, the weakest died," recalled one captive who endured that journey. More than 7,000 prisoners who set out on the Bataan Death March perished before reaching Camp O'Donnell, where scarce resources combined with the hostility and fanaticism of the prison guards made for subhuman conditions that felled half the captives. One later commented that those who perished on the death march were "the lucky ones."

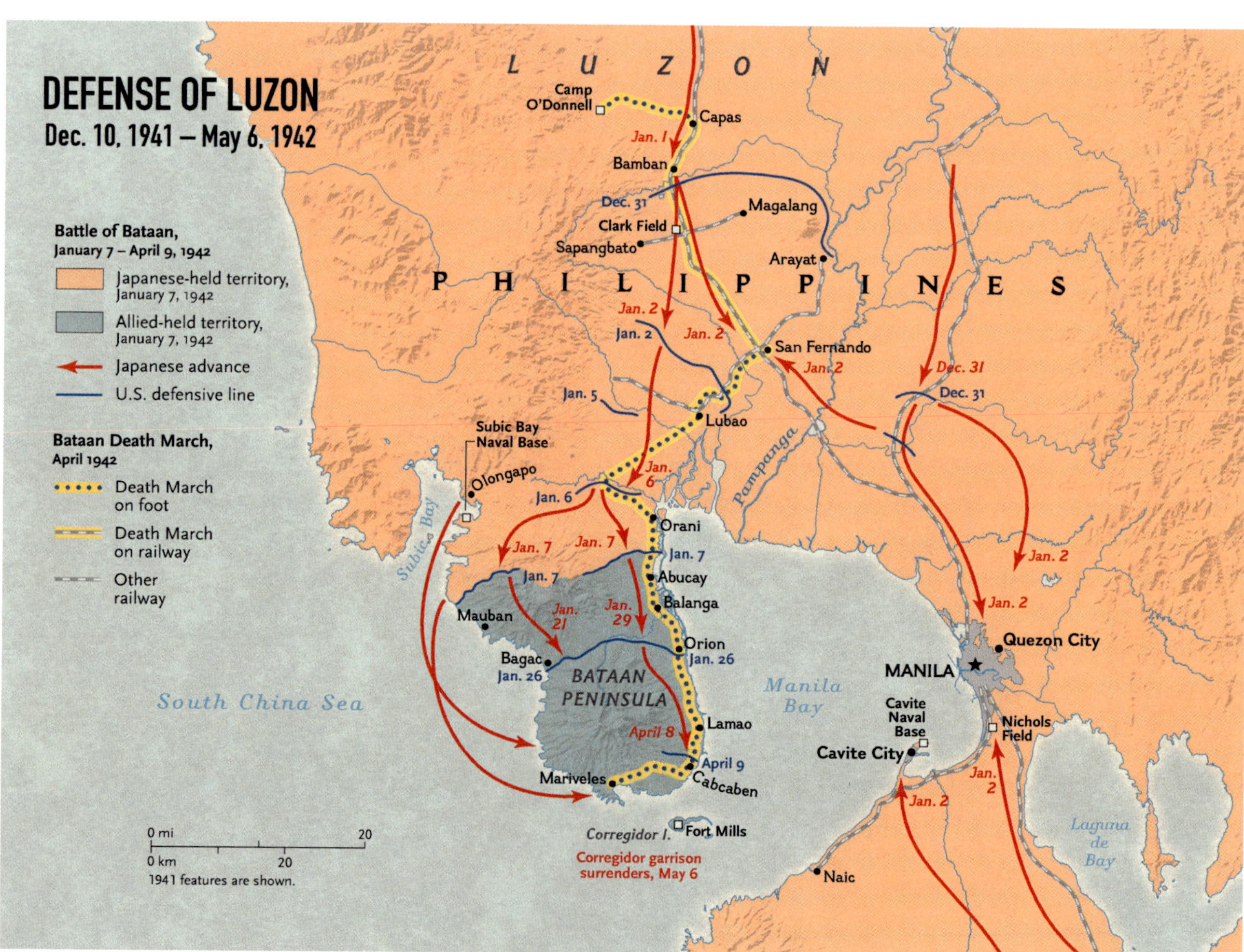

When Japanese troops landed in the Philippines, most of MacArthur's forces—including Filipinos fighting for their country, which had been promised independence by the U.S.—were besieged on Luzon's Bataan Peninsula. Upon surrender, they were subjected to the cruel Bataan Death March during which 7,000 prisoners perished in the walk north to the captured base Camp O'Donnell.

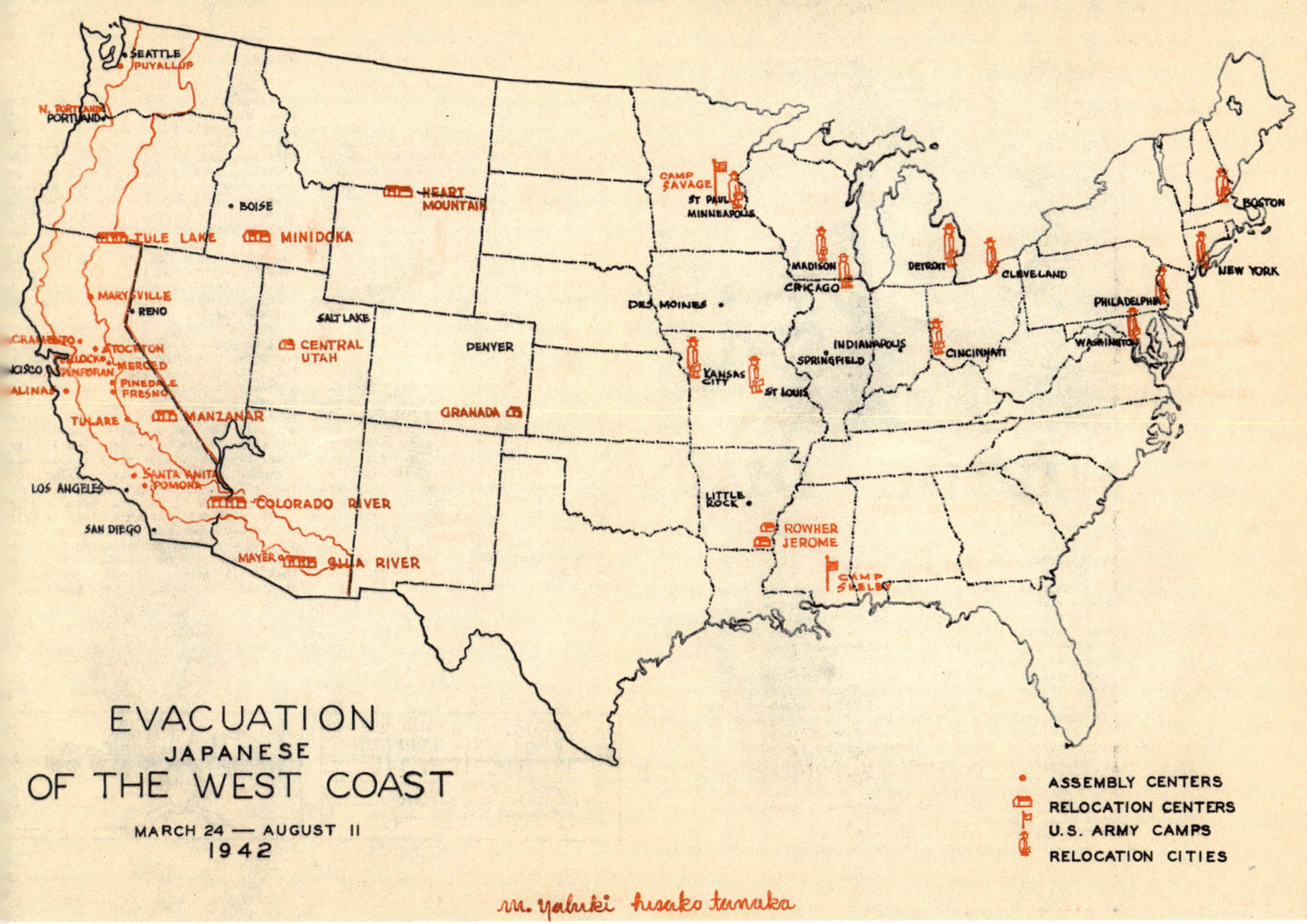

Signed at bottom by the Japanese American who produced it, this map published in 1944 documents the government's drastic internment program.

"I AM AN AMERICAN"

In February 1942, Lt. Gen. John DeWitt, head of the Western Defense Command, recommended removing all Japanese Americans from the West Coast. "The Japanese race is an enemy race," he wrote, adding that those who were "Americanized" had the same "racial strains" as those in Japan. There was no evidence, however, that Japanese Americans were a security threat. As FBI director J. Edgar Hoover put it, their proposed removal was "based primarily upon public and political pressure rather than on factual data." The 400,000 Japanese Americans in Hawaii were too important to the economy to be quarantined. On the West Coast, by contrast, they were a small minority, subject to prejudice that increased after the attack on Pearl Harbor. President Roosevelt ordered the removal of nearly 120,000 Japanese Americans to camps surrounded by barbed wire and watched by armed guards.

The Japanese-American men, women, and children placed in one of 10 internment camps suffered years of indignities and were deprived of housing, resources, and personal liberties. As fears of Japanese subversion receded, authorities began to release and resettle internees. Those who pledged loyalty to the U.S. were eligible for military service, a path chosen by 20,000 Japanese Americans. In the hope of greater assimilation, relocation cities were designated in the East and Midwest. Despite the mistreatment that caused more than 5,000 former internees to return to Japan at war's end, most continued to affirm what one San Franciscan stated before he was detained: "I am an American."

CARRIER WARFARE

+++++++++++++

Before war erupted in the Pacific, battleships "still ruled the waves," wrote Lt. Cmdr. Edwin Layton, chief intelligence officer for the Pacific Fleet. But the attack on Pearl Harbor confirmed that warplanes launched far from aircraft carriers were a major threat to warships. When Adm. Chester Nimitz took charge of the Pacific Fleet, he knew that the aircraft carriers *Enterprise* and *Lexington* mattered more in striking Japan than the battleships the fleet had lost. The return of the U.S.S. *Yorktown* from the Atlantic in January 1942 gave him a third carrier. Admiral Nimitz was willing to risk his carriers in battle because he received intelligence on Admiral Yamamoto's fleet from cryptanalysts cracking the Japanese naval code. Nimitz also had tough skippers eager to avenge Pearl Harbor, like Vice Adm. William "Bull" Halsey, commander of the *Enterprise*, who said of his foes: "Before we're through with them, the Japanese language will be spoken only in hell."

Halsey escorted the U.S.S. *Hornet* on a daring raid against Tokyo. They could not get close enough for conventional carrier-based warplanes, which had a range of about 300 miles (480 km), to hit Tokyo and return. Instead, 16 longer-range B-25 bombers commanded by Lt. Col. James Doolittle of the U.S. Army Air Forces (USAAF) were launched from the *Hornet* at a distance of 670 miles (1,075 km). Too heavy to land on the carries, they dropped their bombs and continued on. Most of the crews landed in friendly Chinese

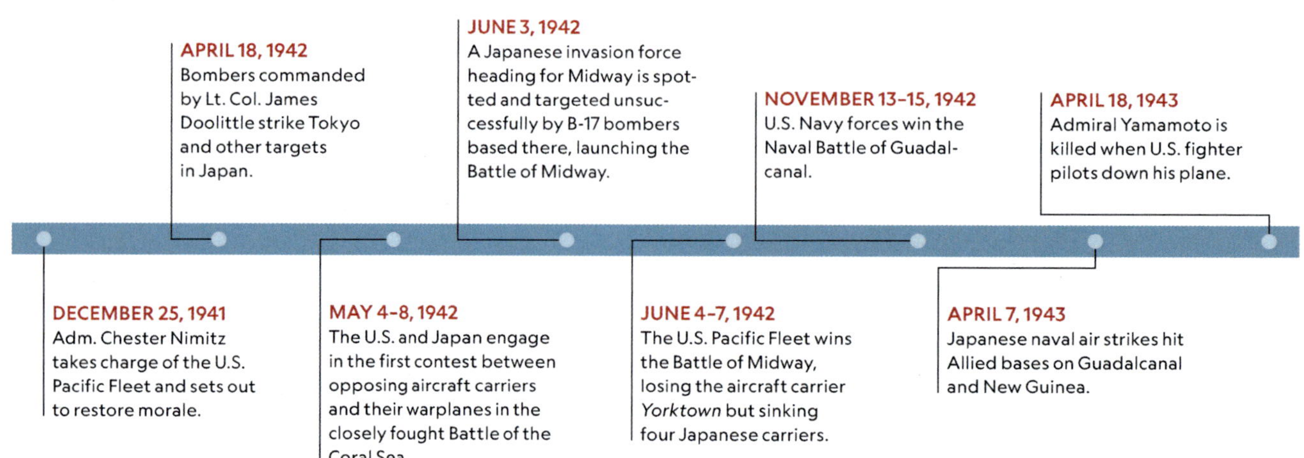

Mapped above are significant battles, raids, or invasions conducted at sea or on land around the Pacific (excluding battles on the Asian mainland) from the start of the Japanese offensive in December 1941 to the death of Admiral Yamamoto in April 1943. The U.S. Navy did not commit aircraft carriers to a series of battles fought around the Dutch East Indies in which Allied naval forces were defeated. But carriers figured prominently in other engagements, including the crucial Battle of Midway in June 1942.

territory, but nine airmen were captured by the Japanese and three were executed. The airstrike troubled Yamamoto, who resolved to extend Japan's defensive perimeter far across the Pacific to American-occupied Midway.

BATTLE OF THE CORAL SEA

Before Admiral Yamamoto launched his Midway offensive, his navy supported the invasions of Port Moresby on Papua and Tulagi, a small island in the lower Solomons that would serve as a naval base while the Japanese built an airfield on Guadalcanal. Two heavy carriers, I.J.N. *Shokaku* and I.J.N. *Zuikaku,* would be deployed if U.S. warships opposed the invasions, and the carrier I.J.N. *Shoho* would lead a covering force assigned to shield Japanese troopships. Analysis of coded Japanese radio signals informed Admiral Nimitz of those deployments, and he dispatched the carriers *Yorktown* and *Lexington,* each with a task force of cruisers and destroyers. Rear Adm. Frank Fletcher on the *Yorktown* had overall command of Task Force 17 as well as Task Force 11, led by Rear Adm. Aubrey Fitch on the *Lexington.* As they entered the Coral Sea, the stage was set for the first battle ever fought between aircraft carriers and their warplanes.

On May 4, 1942, bombers from the *Yorktown* attacked Japanese invasion forces at Tulagi. The *Shokaku* and

Zuikaku approached from the north and sent out scout planes, as did Fletcher's carriers, but cloud cover kept both sides' ships from being spotted until May 7. That morning, Japanese planes sank the destroyer U.S.S. *Sims* and wrecked the oiler U.S.S. *Neosho*. American planes blasted the carrier *Shoho*. On May 8, the Battle of the Coral Sea reached a searing conclusion as the two big carriers on each side launched strikes that damaged the *Shokaku* and *Yorktown* and sank the *Lexington*. The battle proved most costly for Japan. The *Zuikaku* lost so many planes that it soon returned to port with the stricken *Shokaku*. The invasion of Port Moresby was scrubbed, and neither carrier would be available for Yamamoto's assault on Midway a month later.

> "MIDWAY WAS THE MOST CRUCIAL BATTLE OF THE PACIFIC WAR, THE ENGAGEMENT THAT MADE EVERYTHING ELSE POSSIBLE.
>
> – ADM. CHESTER NIMITZ

TURNING POINT AT MIDWAY

Admiral Yamamoto divided his forces for his Midway offensive. He sent a diversionary task force to blast a U.S. base in the Aleutians, where Japanese troops would soon land, and assigned Vice Adm. Chuichi Nagumo's First Air Fleet to bomb Midway before Japanese troops landed there. Yamamoto planned to follow up with reinforcements and hoped to shatter the U.S. Pacific Fleet as it came to Midway's defense. He thought his foes had lost

ABOVE: **Lt. Col. James Doolittle stands at left beside Capt. Marc Mitscher, commanding officer of the U.S.S. *Hornet*, surrounded by pilots and crewmen who would soon raid Tokyo.**

both the *Lexington* and the *Yorktown* in the Coral Sea, but the *Yorktown* made it back to Pearl Harbor and was repaired. That gave Admiral Nimitz three carriers to foil Yamamoto's plans, which code-breakers revealed to him. He sent Task Force 16 under Rear Adm. Raymond Spruance, in charge of the *Enterprise* and *Hornet*, out with Task Force 17 under Rear Admiral Fletcher, who had command on the *Yorktown*. Nimitz figured they had a fighting chance if they got the jump on Nagumo.

U.S. Navy scout planes spotted the Japanese invasion force 700 miles (1,100 km) west of Midway on June 3, 1942, and spotted Nagumo's carriers approaching Midway from the northwest around 5:30 a.m. on June 4. Fletcher ordered Spruance to pursue those carriers and prepared to commit the *Yorktown* to battle. Around 8:30, after withstanding attacks by bombers from Midway, Nagumo learned that one of his own scouts had sighted an enemy carrier. By then, warplanes he had launched earlier against Midway were returning. Nagumo cleared the flight decks for them by ordering planes armed with bombs for a second raid on Midway lowered to the hangar decks and rearmed with torpedoes to target carriers. That process was under way when torpedo planes sent by Spruance attacked. Coming in low, most were downed by enemy fire, but the attack delayed the launch of Nagumo's planes. They were about to take off when dive-bombers from the *Enterprise* and *Yorktown* swooped down at 10:25. Within minutes, Nagumo's flagship, the I.J.N. *Akagi*, and two other carriers, the I.J.N. *Soryu* and I.J.N. *Kaga*, were engulfed in flames. Only the I.J.N. *Hiryu* survived the attack. It was bombed later that day after launching strikes on the *Yorktown*, which eventually sank. Devastated by the outcome, Yamamoto withdrew. As Nimitz later stated, "Midway was the most crucial battle of the Pacific War, the engagement that made everything else possible."

BELOW: **Crewmen prepare to abandon the U.S.S. *Yorktown*, listing after it was torpedoed by planes from the Japanese carrier *Hiryu* on June 4, 1942.**

ISLAND FIGHTING

+++++++++++++

Victory at Midway enabled U.S. forces to challenge Japanese troops for control of islands off eastern Australia, including Guadalcanal in the Solomons. Admiral Nimitz and his staff improved battle readiness of the Pacific Fleet by analyzing serious flaws in the way their forces conducted carrier warfare—a new form of naval combat involving much trial and error. Secret reports on the Battle of Midway noted that heavy losses of torpedo bombers during the attacks demonstrated the "absolute necessity of fighter support" for vulnerable planes, and also pointed out that high-level bombers such as B-17s had little success targeting ships that were intact and capable of taking evasive action, resulting in "mostly 'near misses,' and not near enough."

The Allies' immediate aim was to protect supply lines between the U.S. and Australia, where General MacArthur was preparing for an assault on Papua and New Guinea. In June 1942, Allied coastwatchers spying on Japanese forces, who had occupied Tulagi in May, reported the construction of an airstrip on Guadalcanal from which Japanese bombers could strike ships bound for Australia.

Beginning on August 7, nearly 20,000 U.S. Marines landed on Guadalcanal, Tulagi, and other islands in the vicinity. Supported by ships of the Pacific Fleet and Army forces, they launched the first of many bitter struggles to reclaim territory from Japanese troops,

LEFT: **All five Sullivan brothers—Joseph, Francis, Albert, Madison, and George—perished when the U.S.S. *Juneau* sank at the Naval Battle of Guadalcanal.**

who seldom surrendered. Of the 800 or so occupying Tulagi and other small islands, all but a few dozen died fighting after killing or wounding more than 300 Marines. There was little resistance initially on Guadalcanal, where Navy construction crews called Seabees transformed the airstrip begun by their foes into a U.S. air base, Henderson Field. But Japanese troops delivered by convoy from Rabaul in New Britain launched a furious attack in September at Bloody Ridge, overlooking Henderson Field, where machine-gunners stopped them. "When one wave was mowed down," an American officer recalled, "another wave followed it into death." In October, Marines defending Henderson Field withstood another attack, and Nimitz sent his toughest commander, Bull Halsey, to battle Japanese naval forces and cut off enemy reinforcements.

NAVAL BATTLES OFF THE SOLOMONS

When Admiral Halsey took command of U.S. naval forces in the South Pacific in October 1942, he said it was "the hottest potato" ever handed him. His urgent task was to gain control of the sea-lanes on which troops and supplies reached Guadalcanal. Both sides had suffered heavy losses in those waters since early August, when four Allied cruisers went down off Savo Island in Iron Bottom Sound—so called for the many ships sunk there. Later that month, in the Battle of the Eastern Solomons, Japanese dive-bombers targeted the carrier *Enterprise*, disabling it for two months. Shortly after Halsey took charge, he lost the carrier *Hornet* and the services of the refitted *Enterprise*, damaged in a clash with Japanese carriers off Santa Cruz Island. Halsey rushed repairs on the *Enterprise* and labored to stall the delivery of

Clashes between warships offshore culminated in the Naval Battle of Guadalcanal in November 1942, which led the Japanese to withdraw in early 1943. U.S. forces then invaded New Georgia in July and Bougainville in November, and subjected the Japanese base at Rabaul to air strikes.

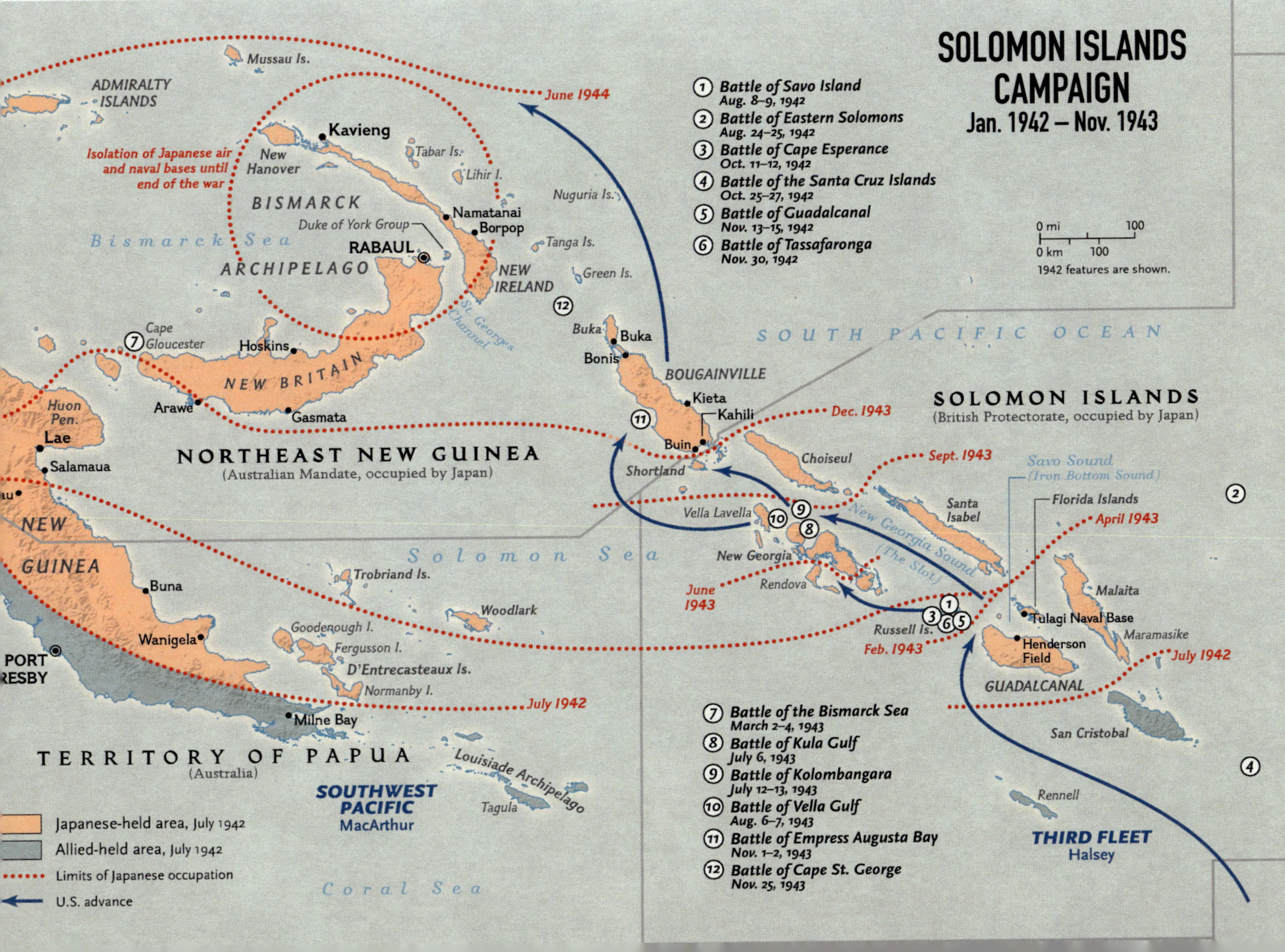

In unfamiliar territory, maps issued to Marines often contained only the bare bones of information that belied the rough terrain of remote Pacific islands. The men filled in the detail with hand-drawn charts and often devised some peculiar place-names and confused some existing place-names. The stream they labeled Alligator Creek was in fact inhabited by crocodiles.

UNCHARTED TERRITORY

The tattered map above sheds light on the first significant battle on Guadalcanal from the perspective of infantry on the ground. Bearing the name of Second Lt. R. R. Binder of the U.S. Marine Corps, it consists of a printed map of the island on the front side, with a hand-drawn chart on the back portraying a crucial area near Lunga Point and the emerging Henderson Field on Guadalcanal's north coast. The airfield was the key reason for the protracted fight for Guadalcanal. On Binder's map and others issued to Marines, the Ilu River was mislabeled the Tenaru River. Hence, the so-called Battle of the Tenaru on August 21, 1942, is sometimes referred to as the Battle of the Ilu. By whatever name, it was a harrowing start to the long, bloody struggle for Guadalcanal.

Japanese Col. Kiyono Ichiki landed on August 19 with some 900 men of his 28th Infantry Regiment on Taivu Point, east of Lunga Point, where Marines were defending the airfield. Ichiki calculated the presence of about 2,000 Marines—the actual number was nearly 10,000—and launched his attack before backup landed. When his men crossed the sandbar at the mouth of the Ilu River around 1 a.m. on the 21st, Marines awaited with rifles, machine guns, and a 37-mm gun loaded with canister that sprayed deadly shrapnel. Their commander, Maj. Gen. Alexander Vandegrift, sent tanks across the sandbar to finish the annihilation. Ichiki reportedly took his own life.

Japanese troops to Guadalcanal by Rear Adm. Raizo Tanaka's fast convoys, known as the Tokyo Express.

In early November, a convoy of two dozen transports and destroyers under Tanaka prepared to advance down the New Georgia Sound and land 12,000 troops on Guadalcanal. Tanaka's convoy was preceded by a bombardment force led by Vice Adm. Hiroaki Abe aboard the battleship I.J.N. *Hiei*, assigned to blast Henderson Field. Around 1:30 a.m. on November 13, Abe's warships encountered a smaller task force led by U.S. Rear Adm. Daniel Callaghan in Iron Bottom Sound. Engaged by Callaghan at close range, Abe's gunners crippled five warships, including the cruiser U.S.S. *Juneau*, which a Japanese submarine later torpedoed and blew up, killing 700 men. Callaghan's forces disabled the *Hiei*, which was sunk by dive-bombers from the *Enterprise*. Spared bombardment, Henderson Field was targeted the following night by cruisers led by Japan's Vice Adm. Gunichi Mikawa. That did not stop bombers there from joining planes from the *Enterprise* in blasting Tanaka's convoy on the 14th and sinking six transports. The Japanese offensive concluded that night when a task force led by U.S. Rear Adm. Willis Lee beat back an attack by Vice Adm. Nobutake Kondo, who lost the battleship I.J.N. *Kirishima* in a duel with the battleships U.S.S. *Washington* and U.S.S. *South Dakota*. Defeat in the Naval Battle of Guadalcanal led the Japanese to withdraw their troops in early 1943.

BATTLES FOR PAPUA

In mid-1942, Japanese commanders targeted Papua, an Australian-held territory. Their main objective was Port Moresby, an Allied stronghold. After plans to invade Port Moresby were disrupted by the U.S. Navy during the Battle of the Coral Sea in May, Japanese troops landed in July around Buna on the far side of Papua and advanced toward Port Moresby on the grueling Kokoda Track over the steep mountains of the Owen Stanley Range. To bolster Australian troops defending Papua, General MacArthur sent reinforcements, including men of the U.S. 32nd Infantry Division. Some of those raw American troops advanced overland as the Japanese fell back to Buna and nearby Gona, where they dug in and resisted fiercely. Other Americans were airlifted over the Owen Stanley Range and rushed into battle at Buna. Many who were not killed or wounded fell ill with malaria, and morale plummeted as the men ran short of food.

In late November, MacArthur sent Lt. Gen. Robert Eichelberger to Papua to rally the troops. "Bob," MacArthur briefed him, "I want you to take Buna, or not come back alive." Eichelberger understood that he and his men would have to match the "do or die" Japanese mindset in battle. After ensuring that his soldiers were

ABOVE: **A Papuan leads an Australian soldier he found blinded in a thicket to safety at an Allied camp. Papuans frequently aided Australian and American troops.**

"BOB, I WANT YOU TO TAKE BUNA, OR NOT COME BACK ALIVE."

—GEN. DOUGLAS MACARTHUR TO LT. GEN. ROBERT EICHELBERGER

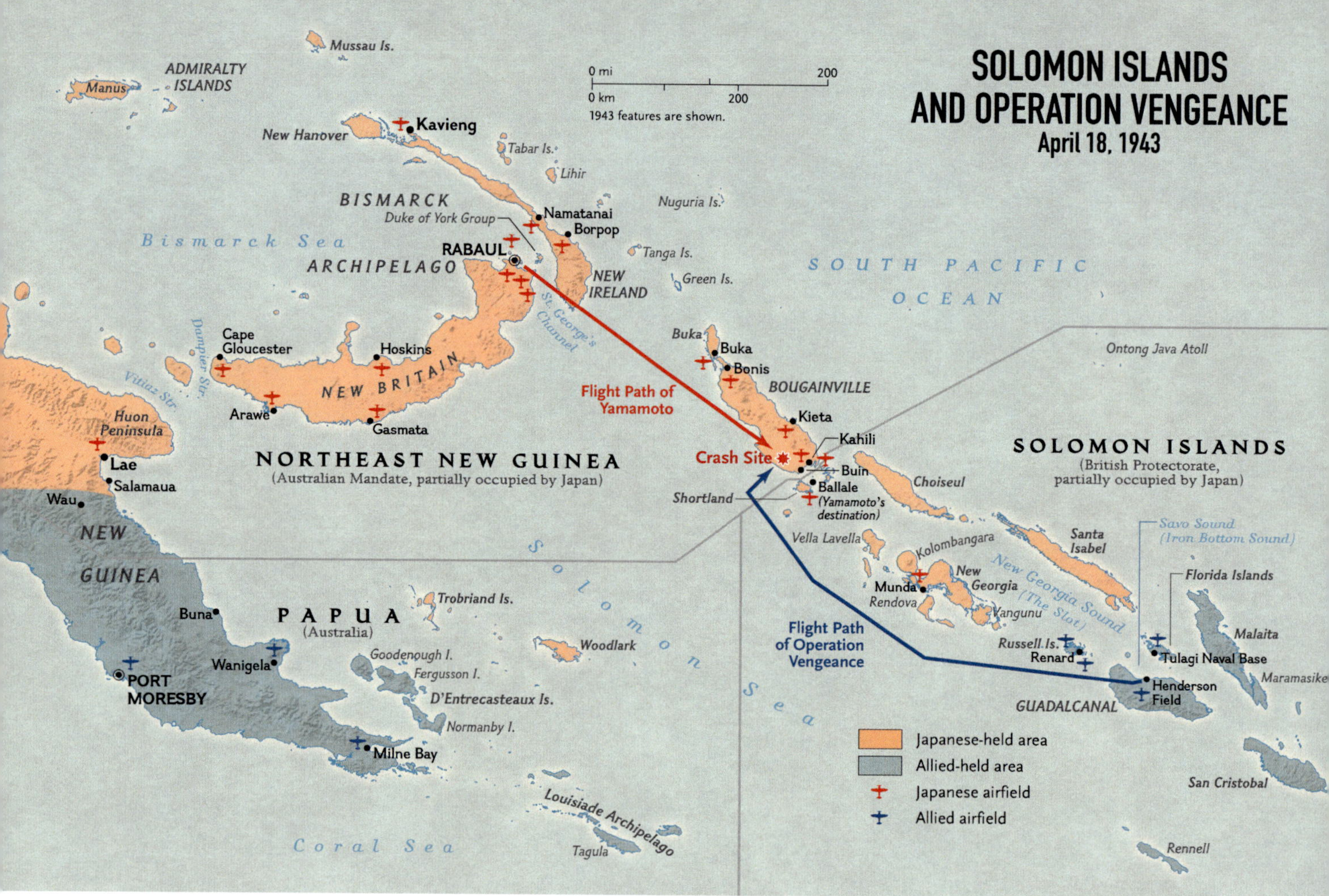

On April 18, 1943, Admiral Yamamoto departed from the Japanese base at Rabaul. Alerted by his deciphered itinerary, American fighter pilots took off from Henderson Field and followed the path traced here to Bougainville, where they downed Yamamoto's plane, killing Yamamoto and accomplishing a mission dubbed Operation Vengeance.

well led and well fed, he launched a determined assault on enemy lines at Buna while Australians attacked at Gona and at nearby Sanananda with some American support. By late December, Japanese defenses were crumbling. "Rotting bodies, sometimes weeks old," formed part of their fortifications, a journalist noted. In early January 1943, American and Australian troops took Buna. By month's end, the battle for Papua was over—a costly Allied victory that left much fighting to be done before MacArthur secured New Guinea and could return to the Philippines.

DOWNING YAMAMOTO

Before the war began, Admiral Yamamoto said that if Japan took on the United States, his fleet would "run wild for the first six months or a year, but I have utterly no confidence for the second or third year." By 1943, that conflict was in its second year and the Pacific Fleet was growing at a pace Yamamoto's fleet could not match. Hoping to thwart enemy advances in the southwest Pacific, he flew on April 3 to the Japanese base at Rabaul on New Britain to launch Operation I-Go, involving naval air strikes against Allied bases on Guadalcanal and Papua. Those attacks did not surprise his opponents. Since Pearl Harbor, American forces had greatly enhanced their ability to anticipate raids, using techniques known to the Japanese such as radar and other more recently developed methods that even Yamamoto, well aware of American technological prowess, did not envision. U.S. Navy code-breakers, aided by machines that were forerunners of digital computers, could now decipher Japanese radio messages fast enough to wreck enemy plans.

On April 13, Yamamoto's enciphered itinerary for his

flight on the 18th to visit three Japanese bases around Bougainville in the Solomons was broadcast to officers there. Within 36 hours, cryptanalysts at Pearl Harbor had deciphered most of that itinerary. Admiral Nimitz agreed with Commander Layton's intelligence assessment that "shooting down Yamamoto would be a vital and serious blow to the Japanese," and received permission from Washington to order an attack by pilots from Henderson Field on Guadalcanal. Led by Maj. John Mitchell of the USAAF, they took off at 7:10 a.m. on April 18 in P-38 Lightnings, swift fighters equipped with drop tanks to extend their range, and flew low over the Coral Sea to avoid detection by radar. Capt. Thomas Lanphier, Jr., was assigned to lead the "killer flight" of four P-38s that would target Yamamoto's bomber while other pilots dueled with fighters escorting the admiral. At 9:45, they intercepted Yamamoto's flight off Bougainville and sent his plane crashing into the jungle, where a Japanese search party later found his body amid the wreckage. Yamamoto's death was a bitter blow for Japan, which now faced an agonizing struggle to stave off defeat. ■

ABOVE: **Capt. Thomas Lanphier, Jr., is pictured standing at right beside Lt. Rex Barber, with whom he shared credit for downing Yamamoto.** BELOW: **Lanphier sketched the path they followed on April 18, 1943, in a journal entry. After swinging west of the Solomons to avoid detection, they returned safely to Henderson Field.**

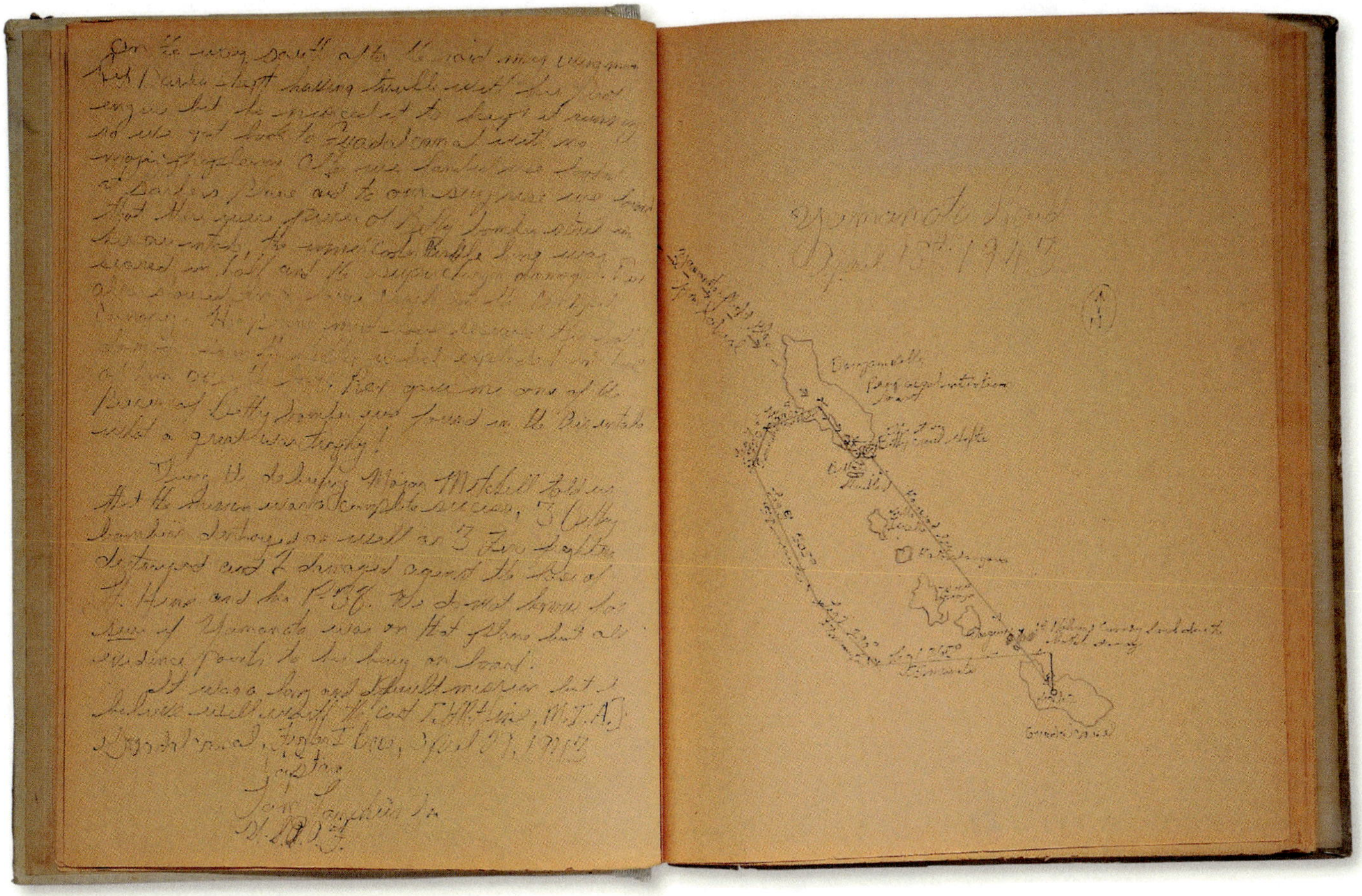

British commandos of the Special Air Service carry Vickers aircraft machine guns for a raid behind Axis lines in North Africa.

CHAPTER 3

BREAKING HITLER'S GRIP

1942-1944

By 1942, Hitler controlled much of Europe, which Germans labeled Festung Europa (Fortress Europe). "Never use that term again," snapped Winston Churchill when a British commander referred to "Hitler's European Fortress." Churchill planned to penetrate occupied Europe and open a second front to relieve pressure on Soviet troops fighting in the East. Unwilling to risk invasion in 1942, he urged President Roosevelt to commit American troops to North Africa, where the British faced armored forces led by Erwin Rommel. U.S. Army chief George Marshall feared that Churchill's Mediterranean strategy would delay an advance into Germany through France. But the assault on Fortress Europe would have to wait until the Allies achieved air superiority and won the Battle of the Atlantic, where U-boats menaced Allied supply lines.

In mid-1942, German forces regained momentum in Russia and advanced in North Africa toward Cairo. Later that year, the tide turned. British and Commonwealth troops won the Battle of El Alamein in occupied Egypt, Anglo-American forces seized French North Africa from Vichy authorities, and the Soviets annihilated a German army at Stalingrad in early 1943. In July, Allied troops crossed from Tunisia to Sicily, toppling Mussolini. The grueling Italian campaign tied down German troops while Allied forces prepared to invade France; it also provided bases for warplanes that blasted Axis cities and degraded the Luftwaffe. A British leaflet dropped on the Reich, where air raids continued, declared: "Fortress Europe Has No Roof." Before long, the fortress walls would be breached as Russians advanced in the east and D-Day approached in the west.

JANUARY 1, 1942
Twenty-three Allied governments sign the Declaration of the United Nations.

JANUARY 20, 1942
SS officer Reinhard Heydrich holds the Wannsee Conference on the "Final Solution," a plan kill European Jews.

JUNE 21, 1942
Gen. Erwin Rommel seizes Tobruk, Libya, which will serve as a supply base as he invades Egypt.

NOVEMBER 4, 1942
Rommel concedes defeat at the Second Battle of El Alamein in Egypt, routed by Montgomery's British Eighth Army.

MAY 7, 1943
Allied troops capture Tunis, the last Axis bastion in Tunisia.

JULY 27-28, 1943
RAF bombers ignite a firestorm in Hamburg, Germany, where more than 40,000 people are killed.

NOVEMBER 17, 1943
Treblinka extermination camp closes following the execution of more than 780,000 people there. Killings continue at Auschwitz and other Nazi camps.

NOVEMBER 22-23, 1943
RAF Bomber Command blasts Berlin, causing extensive damage.

NOVEMBER 28, 1943
Roosevelt, Churchill, and Stalin meet in Tehran to schedule an Allied invasion of German-occupied France for spring of 1944.

DEFIANCE AND REPRESSION

+++++++++++++

By 1940, German forces had overrun Norway, Denmark, Holland, Belgium, and France, leading to years of strife as civilians resisted occupation and risked execution. In France, 600,000 men were forced to labor in Germany or build the Atlantic Wall—coastal fortifications against an Allied invasion. Vichy authorities in southern France collaborated with the occupiers, and French police helped SS officers round up Jews and track down Communists and partisans. In August 1942, Communists hurled grenades at Luftwaffe airmen attending a soccer match in Paris, killing three and wounding others. Germans retaliated by executing 88 hostages, including 14 workers for the resistance newspaper *L'Humanité*.

Repression was even fiercer in some countries that Germany annexed. In Poland, the SS set out to kill all opposing officers and influential figures, but a large underground resistance movement called the Polish Home Army pushed back. In the Protectorate of Bohemia and Moravia, several thousand people were executed in retaliation for the death of SS security chief Reinhard Heydrich, who was killed in June 1942 by Czech commandos trained by the SOE (Special Operations Executive) in Britain. Allied agencies also supported networks that helped downed pilots in occupied Europe escape. Marseille and Lyon, in Vichy France, were hotbeds of resistance where those wanted by the Nazis found refuge. But after German troops occupied the Vichy zone in November 1942, few places other than remote rural areas were safe.

CARTE D'IDENTITÉ

Nom: Pailly
Prénoms: René
Profession: Voyageur
N. le 5 Juin 1915 Tréboul
Département: du Finistère
Nationalité: Française
Domicile: rue de la Tour d'Auvergne à Tréboul

DA 13 FRANCS

SIGNALEMENT

Taille: 1 m 70
Cheveux: Chatain clair
Moustache:
Yeux: Bleus
Nez: (Dos) ordinaire; (Base) rect.; (Dimensions) Forte
Forme du visage: Ovale
Teint: Mat
Signes particuliers:
Empreinte digitale
Le Titulaire: R. Pailly
Les Témoins:
Vu pour légalisation
Le 23 MARS 1942

LEFT: **A forged identity card for a French resistance fighter**

By December 1941, much of Europe had been occupied, absorbed, or drawn into the Axis by Germany, which kept a tight hold on France and other nations along the Atlantic to prevent Allied forces from invading there. None of the neutral countries threatened the Reich's continental dominance.

ESCAPE LINES TO FREEDOM

More than 55,000 of the 120,000 men who served in the RAF Bomber Command were killed, and nearly 10,000 were captured. But some 5,000 Allied airmen shot down in occupied Europe escaped. Most escape lines originated in Belgium or northern France along the flight paths of Allied bombers. The Comet Line was organized by Andrée "Dédée" de Jongh of Belgium, aided by her father and others who arranged safe houses and furnished airmen with civilian clothing and counterfeit documents. This network relied on skilled forgers who kept up with frequent changes made in German documents. Conductors guided the airmen to neutral Spain, where British officials quietly arranged a return to Britain via Gibraltar.

MI9, a British agency established to help servicemen in enemy territory escape, funded the Comet Line and sustained the O'Leary Line, led by Albert-Marie Guérisse, a Belgian who had been evacuated from Dunkirk to England, where he took the name Patrick O'Leary. In mid-1942, O'Leary and MI9 opened a new route evacuating escapees by ship at night along the Mediterranean coast of Vichy France. The German occupation of the Vichy zone ended that operation and imperiled resistance efforts in Marseille, where O'Leary was based. The Gestapo arrested O'Leary in March 1943. He survived confinement in a concentration camp, as did Dédée de Jongh, seized in January.

The Comet Line continued under new leadership, and new escape lines included the Shelburne Line, established by MI9 in late 1943 to help downed airmen escape across the English Channel from northwest France. Hundreds in occupied Europe lost their lives so that stranded airmen could reach freedom.

COMBATING THE U-BOAT PERIL

+++++++++++++

For Vice Adm. Karl Dönitz, commander in chief of the German U-boat fleet, America's entry into the war offered an opportunity to instigate the crucial battle for control of the Atlantic and the maritime supply lines on which Allied hopes rested. The British had reduced losses in the North Atlantic by neutralizing Germany's surface fleet—which pulled back after the vaunted battleship *Bismarck* was sunk in May 1941—and by organizing armed naval convoys that shielded merchant ships against U-boats. Ships in American coastal waters, however, went unescorted and were highly vulnerable to attack. Beginning in January 1942, when Dönitz launched Operation Drumbeat, U-boats wreaked havoc off American shores. U-boat captains called it their "Second Happy Time," the first having ended when the heavily defended transatlantic convoys were instituted.

ADVANCES IN U-BOAT TECHNOLOGIES

Capt. Reinhard Hardegan, one of the first U-boat commanders sent by Admiral Dönitz to sink ships off the North American coast, departed so soon after Germany declared war on the U.S. that he lacked charts of the waters in which he would operate. Hardegan relied instead on an "old student tourist guide," he recalled, and "used it to navigate along the coast." Captains who followed in his aggressive path were aided by official maps, including tidal and depth charts—vital information for U-boats that often operated close to shore, sometimes entering waters too shallow to allow them to submerge if they came under attack. Various instruments also aided them in charting their position at night by stars and target ships.

The German Navy was also greatly advantaged by new developments in submarine targeting weaponry. For example, the hand-operated torpedo-firing calculator, which computed when to fire based on factors such as the target's estimated speed and distance, was replaced on many U-boats during World War II by an

> [THE] ONLY THING THAT EVER REALLY FRIGHTENED ME DURING THE WAR WAS THE U-BOAT PERIL.
>
> —WINSTON CHURCHILL, BRITISH PRIME MINISTER

Allied merchant ship losses prior to 1942 (yellow dots) were concentrated around the British Isles. Merchant ship losses thereafter (green dots) spread far across the Atlantic as U-boats expanded their range. In 1943, Allied air patrols (shaded areas) and other defensive measures caused steep U-boat losses (red dots) in the North Atlantic, ending the critical threat to supply lines there.

electromechanical computer that pulled data from the captain's attack periscope to calculate when to fire with enhanced accuracy. Such innovative technology made the long-range Type IX U-boats deployed in Operation Drumbeat that much deadlier when they stalked America's Northeast coast, targeting such key strategic ports as Portsmouth Harbor on the New Hampshire–Maine border, site of the Portsmouth Naval Shipyard.

THE AMERICAN SHOOTING SEASON

On January 11, 1942, German captain Hardegan struck the first blow in Operation Drumbeat when his *U-123* sank the British freighter *Cyclops* off the coast of Nova Scotia, resulting in the death of 87 crewmen. Hardegan's Type IX was one of five such U-boats that Dönitz committed to the operation, which ranged from the Canadian Maritimes to North Carolina's Cape Hatteras. The target area on the coast of North America was divided into quadrants marked with code—a more secure system for locating navy vessels in wartime than if they communicated using degrees of latitude and longitude. Collectively, the five commanders and their crews sank merchant ships at an alarming rate of roughly one a day before returning to base in early February. Hunting mainly at night, they exploited the fact that blackouts had not yet been imposed in the United States, enabling them to spot the silhouettes of freighters backlit by the glow of New York and other coastal cities. Many ships went down within sight of shore.

Dönitz followed up Operation Drumbeat by sending several additional waves of U-boats across the Atlantic to prowl in American waters, including shorter-range Type VIIs that were refueled in mid-ocean by supply boats called "milk cows." With more forces deployed, he extended their range southward from Cape Hatteras to

ABOVE: **Two German long-range Type IX U-boats surface during Operation Drumbeat in early 1942.** OPPOSITE: **Torpedo strikes—as photographed through this U-boat periscope—ignited fierce explosions on Allied oil tankers.**

the Caribbean and into the Gulf of Mexico. Among their prime targets were oil tankers—floating tinderboxes that when struck by torpedoes erupted in smoke and flames with deadly consequences. During the first six months of 1942, nearly 400 ships were sunk at a cost of some 5,000 lives. U-boat officers called it the "American Shooting Season." By July 1942, however, their depredations were diminishing as blackouts took effect along the coast, aerial surveillance increased, and convoys were organized. Dönitz began withdrawing U-boats from American waters to step up attacks on Allied supply lines in mid-ocean, where the Battle of the Atlantic was approaching its climax.

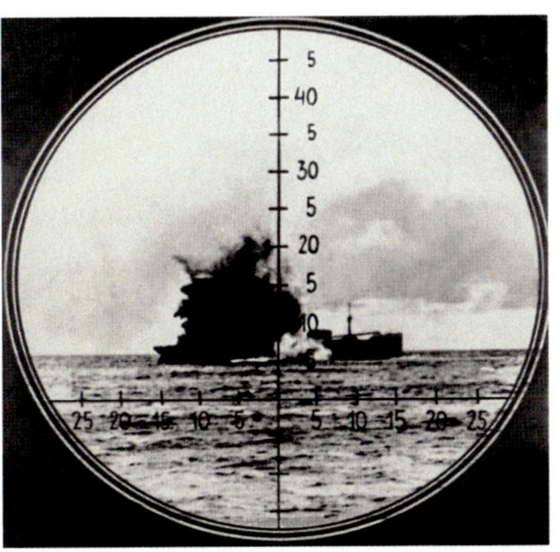

Allied shipping losses in the mid-Atlantic increased alarmingly in the spring of 1942 after the German Navy enhanced the Enigma machine used to encipher its signals, including directives sent from headquarters to coordinate the movements of U-boats that hunted in wolf packs. Messages revealing the whereabouts of those packs and enabling convoys to evade them could no longer be promptly deciphered at Bletchley Park, Britain's top secret code-breaking facility. These were tense times for Winston Churchill, who wrote later that the "only thing that ever really frightened me during the war was the U-boat peril." By year's end, however, wizards at Bletchley had solved the enhanced naval Enigma using coding documents captured from a U-boat that was attacked and boarded. That breakthrough, combined with technological advances in antisubmarine warfare, turned the tide of the Battle of the Atlantic decisively in favor of the Allies. U-boat crews would continue to launch attacks sporadically until war's end, but their happy times were over. ■

SOLVING THE ENIGMA

Between May and November 1942, U-boats sank more than 900 ships, nearly three times the number sank in the same period a year earlier. U-boats were now equipped with Enigma cipher machines containing four rotors (see left), rather than three, and that multiplied exponentially the number of possible settings. This stumped cryptanalysts at Bletchley Park, who had solved the three-rotor Enigma in 1941, with the help of "pinches," including one Enigma machine recovered from the disabled *U-110* by sailors from the destroyer H.M.S. *Bulldog*.

When the four-rotor Enigma entered service, preventing code-breakers from deciphering U-boat messages, another pinch was needed. This occurred in the Mediterranean on October 30, 1942, when three men from the destroyer H.M.S. *Petard* swam to the abandoned *U-559*. Lt. Anthony Fasson and Able Seaman Colin Grazier entered, grabbed documents, and passed them to Tommy Brown, who escaped as the U-boat sank with the two men aboard. The documents they died for included a manual to encode weather reports before they were enciphered. Knowing this weather code, cryptanalysts broke the Enigma cipher. This new intelligence, combined with innovations like Huff Duff—high-frequency radio direction finders that fixed on signals from subs—helped sink so many U-boats that Dönitz withdrew his fleet from the North Atlantic in May 1943. The Allies had won the Battle of the Atlantic.

WAR IN THE DESERT

+++++++++++++

Gen. Erwin Rommel understood the ebb and flow of desert war, a pattern set in North Africa since September 1940, when troops from Italian-held Libya invaded British-ruled Egypt, making rapid gains before being outflanked. Some 200,000 Italian soldiers retreated in disarray. Many became prisoners of war before Hitler dispatched Rommel to Libya. Known as the "Desert Fox" for cunning maneuvers that sent British forces reeling in 1941, Rommel advanced across Libya to the Egyptian border with his armored Afrika Korps. But his opponents clung to Tobruk—denying Rommel a key port—and pushed him into retreat. By January 1942, Rommel was back at El Agheila in Libya, where he had launched his North African campaign the previous March.

Furnished with additional tanks and troops, Rommel saw the British were overextended and set out once again to conquer Egypt and the Suez Canal, which would bring North Africa and the Middle East under Axis or Vichy rule. Unanticipated in his strategy was that U.S. troops would invade Morocco and Algeria in November 1942, and Rommel's army would be caught between the oncoming Yanks and their British allies.

ROMMEL'S BIG PUSH

On January 21, 1942, Rommel advanced from El Agheila against the British Eighth Army, led by Maj. Gen. Neil Ritchie and Gen. Claude Auchinleck, British commander in chief in the Middle East. Auchinleck's strength was reduced as assets were relocated to combat the Japanese in the Far East. Also, German U-boats had entered the Mediterranean to target convoys that supplied the Eighth Army, which was ill equipped to defend

LEFT: **Renowned for leading from the front, Rommel crosses the desert in Libya, equipped with captured British goggles to keep dust out of his eyes.**

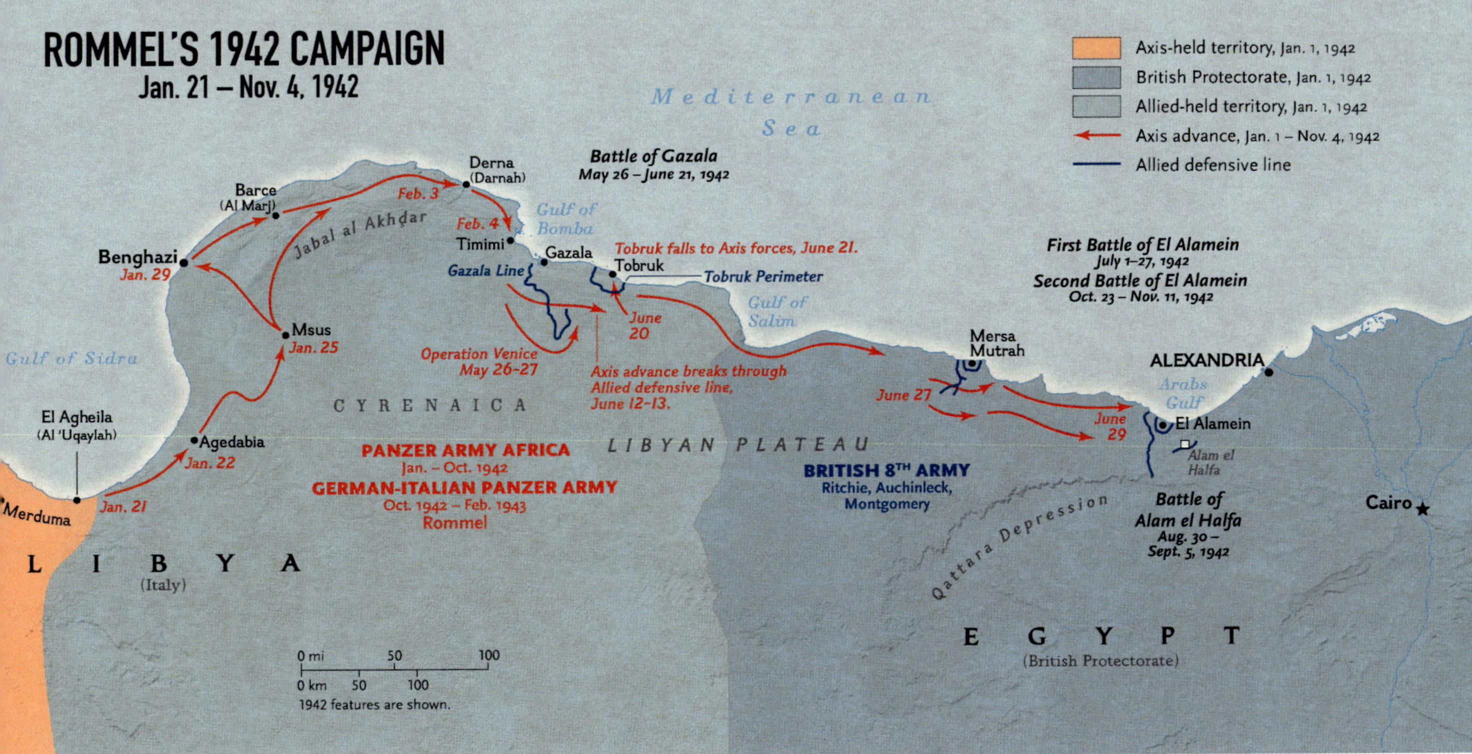

In 1942, Rommel shattered the Gazala Line, captured Tobruk, and invaded Egypt before encountering concerted British opposition at El Alamein.

the ground gained in Libya in late 1941. Rommel's army—aided by Italian units—had by then seized Benghazi and forced Ritchie's troops to withdraw to a fortified line extending southward from the Mediterranean coast near Gazala.

Rommel attacked the Gazala Line in May, aided by the Luftwaffe, which pounded the southernmost stronghold. Ritchie's forces were outflanked but clawed their way out. Auchinleck proposed to withdraw his forces from Libya. But Churchill insisted that Tobruk be defended. "Tobruk was a symbol of British resistance," Rommel later wrote, "and we were now going to finish with it for good." Blasted from the air on June 20, the port fell a day later to Rommel, who gained a supply base for his advance into Egypt. Promoted to field marshal by Hitler, Rommel wrote his wife: "I would much rather that he had given me one more division."

BATTLE LINES DRAWN IN EGYPT

The loss of Tobruk was a blow for the British. Auchinleck took command of the Eighth Army, which he withdrew to a defensive line in Egypt between El Alamein and the Qattara Depression, whose sand dunes, marshes, and salt flats were impenetrable by Rommel's tanks. During the First Battle of El Alamein, in July 1942, Auchinleck held his ground. But Churchill ousted him as Middle East commander in favor of Lt. Gen. Harold Alexander and placed the Eighth Army under Lt. Gen. Bernard "Monty" Montgomery. Alexander met with Monty in Cairo and gave him a succinct order: "Go down to the desert and defeat Rommel."

The British were now close to their supply base at Alexandria, whereas Rommel's supply lines were stretched and vulnerable. The British sank 100 Axis ships in the Mediterranean between January and August

> TOBRUK WAS A SYMBOL OF BRITISH RESISTANCE AND WE WERE NOW GOING TO FINISH WITH IT FOR GOOD.
>
> —GERMAN COL. GEN. ERWIN ROMMEL

1942, many of them carrying oil and armaments for Rommel's forces. Supplies that reached Libya were targeted by the Allied Desert Air Force when in transit overland to El Alamein. Eager to attack while his panzers were well fueled, Rommel attempted to penetrate the southern end of the British line in August. Informed of that plan, Monty allowed some of Rommel's panzers to get as far as Alam el Halfa, where they ground to a halt under blistering fire. When that battle ended on September 5, Rommel went on the defensive while Montgomery planned a bruising, head-on attack at El Alamein.

BREAKTHROUGH AT EL ALAMEIN

As battle loomed at El Alamein in October 1942, Montgomery received intelligence on the dwindling supplies and ill health of Rommel, who flew to Germany for treatment in September. Command passed to Gen. Georg Stumme, who was taken in by elaborate British deceptions indicating that Monty would attack at the southern end of the line in November. When the battle opened with a thunderous artillery barrage on October 23, and British sappers began clearing mines for an attack at the northern end near El Alamein Station, Stumme suffered a fatal heart attack.

Rommel returned on October 25 to find Montgomery's forces on the verge of a breakthrough in the north. By throwing the 21st and 15th Panzer Divisions into that fight, Rommel averted disaster. But he was left with too few resources to overcome Operation Supercharge, a furious assault at the center of the line on November 2. Infantry led the way, followed by British armored divisions, which pressed Rommel's depleted panzers to the

ABOVE: **German soldiers struggle to march across windblown sand dunes near El Alamein in 1942.**

breaking point. Rommel turned in retreat on November 4 and was pushed out of Egypt on November 11.

OPERATION TORCH

The Allied invasion of French North Africa, Operation Torch, was led by Lt. Gen. Dwight D. Eisenhower, and carried out largely by American troops. "This is an American enterprise in which we are your help mates," Churchill told Roosevelt. FDR knew that Americans were less likely to be opposed by Vichy French forces than the British, who had attacked the French fleet in July 1940. French resistance was sporadic when Allied troops landed at multiple points in Morocco and Algeria in November 1942. The Vichy commander in North Africa, Adm. Jean Darlan, soon agreed to a cease-fire. Maj. Gen George Patton knew that green American troops landing in Morocco had been fortunate. Had they been "opposed by Germans," he stated, "we never would have gotten ashore."

The real test came in Tunisia when American armored forces faced Rommel's panzers—who were pursued by Montgomery's Eighth Army—and Gen. Hans-Jürgen von Arnim's Fifth Panzer Army, which landed at Tunis. Fortified with two of Arnim's panzer divisions, Rommel scorched the U.S. II Corps at Kasserine Pass in February 1943, before determined resistance from British infantry backed by artillery and anti-tank units of the U.S. Ninth Division induced him to pull back. Following that costly battle, Eisenhower sent the hard-driving Patton to whip II Corps into shape while Montgomery's army drove Axis forces into a trap around Tunis. Hitler refused to evacuate them and had more troops airlifted there. In early May, the revived II Corps descended on Bizerte, while Allied troops closed in from the south. By then, the ailing Rommel had returned to Germany, leaving Arnim in charge. On May 7, he surrendered, bringing the long struggle for control of North Africa to a close. ■

On November 8, Allied task forces landed in Morocco and Algeria. General Patton proceeded with the invasion by his Western Task Force after receiving a coded message from Eisenhower to "play ball." Vichy French commanders soon yielded to Operation Torch.

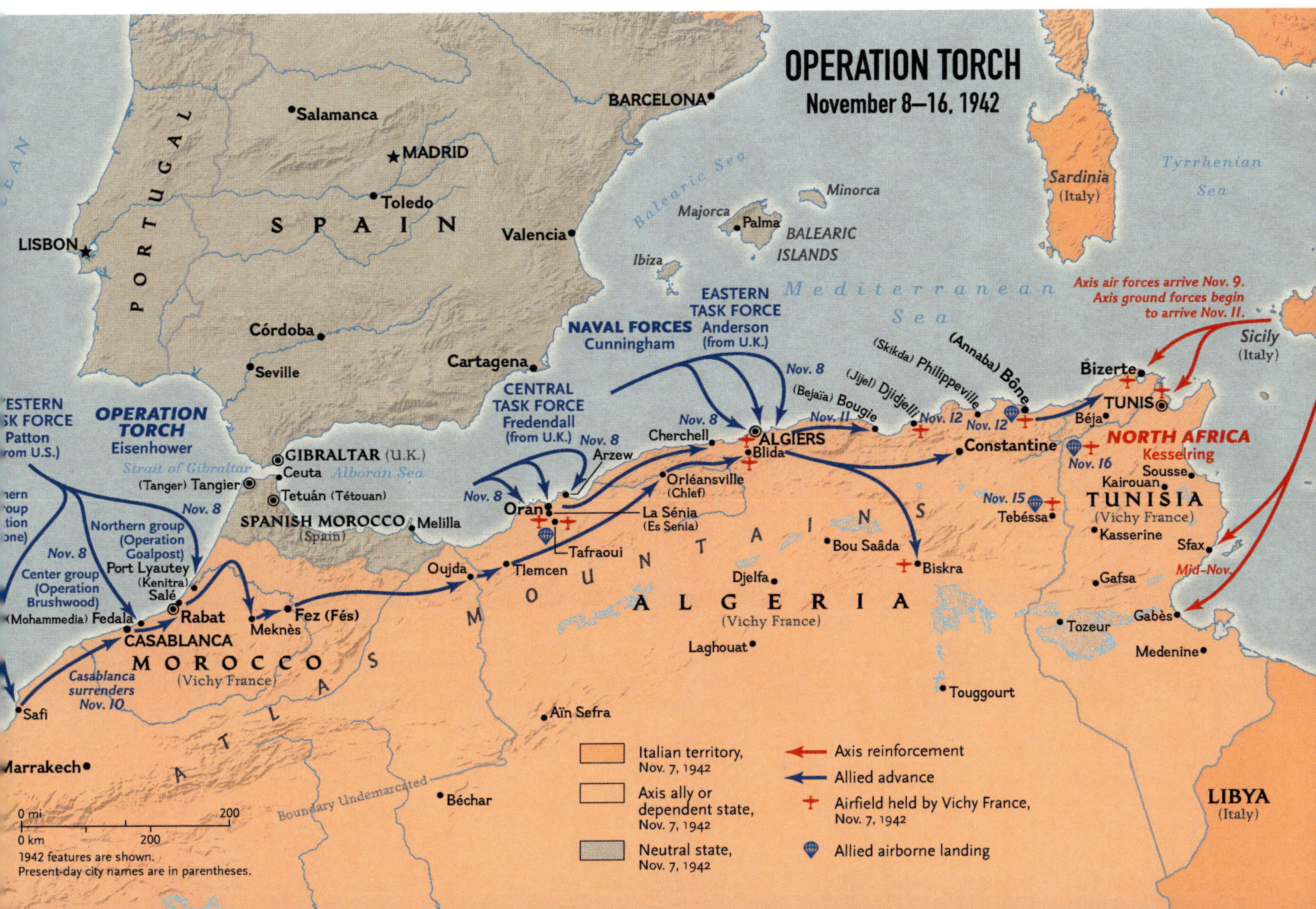

THE ITALIAN CAMPAIGN

In 1943, the British proposed advancing from North Africa to Sicily and on to mainland Italy led by the Fascist militant Benito Mussolini. U.S. Army general Marshall argued for invading France, not Italy, which he viewed as a hard target with steep terrain. Germany was shielded from Italy by neutral Switzerland and the towering Alps, he reasoned. After much debate, Marshall joined President Roosevelt and General Eisenhower in approving a campaign to take Italy and tie down German divisions there prior to the invasion of France, planned for 1944.

For the invasion of Sicily, code-named Operation Husky, more than 3,000 ships and landing craft assembled on the coast of Tunisia to convey 80,000 troops to the island. Before the first troops came ashore at dawn on July 10, 1943, airborne forces landed behind Axis lines to seize roads, bridges, and other targets. General Patton then engaged in a "horse race" between his Seventh Army and the British Eighth Army as both forces advanced toward the final prize of Messina. Patton won, but many Axis troops escaped to the mainland, where the Allies faced a long and grueling struggle.

BRITISH LANDINGS

Operation Husky was an enormous amphibious operation; more Allied divisions landed in Sicily on July 10 than came ashore on D-Day. Meticulous planning and daring reconnaissance went into the making of Husky invasion

maps, outlining landing zones for the British Eighth Army. Before the invasion, COPPs (Combined Operations Pilotage Parties) were launched at night from submarines off Sicily's coast and paddled ashore in folding boats to reconnoiter eastern beaches. Landing sites were charted in great detail, allowing Royal Navy Beach Commandos to secure each site and direct landing craft.

Montgomery's Eighth Army quickly took Syracuse and advanced toward Messina, where his troops met with mounting German resistance as they approached Mount Etna. The Germans extended their Etna Line across the island. Not until mid-August did the Eighth Army break through. By then, Field Marshal Albert Kesselring, had decided to withdraw German troops from Messina before Montgomery or Patton could reach that port.

ALLIED ADVANCES IN SOUTHERN ITALY

Disgraced by the loss of Sicily, Mussolini was deposed and arrested by his compatriots on July 25, 1943. His successor, Field Marshal Pietro Badoglio, entered secret talks with the Allies. Hitler sent seven German divisions to northern Italy and authorized an operation to free Mussolini. In August, Kesselring's German troops withdrew toward Salerno, a likely landing zone for an Allied advance on Naples and Rome. Montgomery's Eighth Army landed with ease at Reggio di Calabria on September 3. But Kesselring's withdrawal spelled trouble for Operation Avalanche, led by Lt. Gen. Mark Wayne Clark and his U.S. Fifth Army, which included the British X Corps.

Clark's forces landed at Salerno on September 9 and came under fire from planes, tanks, and artillery. Clark's decision to land British and American troops on opposite sides of a river entering the Gulf of Salerno left him hamstrung when German armored forces attacked the American sector on the 13th. Reinforced by the 82nd Airborne and the U.S. 45th Infantry Division and aided by Allied air strikes, Clark's troops hit back and held out until the Eighth Army arrived. The Germans withdrew

ABOVE: **An American soldier receives blood plasma from a medic in July 1943, watched by Sicilians. Many islanders had lost faith in Mussolini.**

north of Naples. The Allies entered that city on October 1 to find docks wrecked, water and sewage systems destroyed, and the ruins mined. Hard fighting lay ahead as the Allies entered the Apennine Mountains and confronted the German Gustav Line (Winter Line), which barred their way to Rome.

COLLISION AT CASSINO

Perched high above the town of Cassino, the Benedictine monastery on Monte Cassino was caught in the crosshairs when Clark's Fifth Army targeted the Gustav Line in early 1944. That German barrier included fortified artillery and machine-gun posts on high ground overlooking rivers that Clark's troops had to cross to reach Rome, 80 miles (130 km) away. Big guns on Monte Cassino and minefields in the valleys made advances so perilous that the Allies sought to skirt that line by landing at Anzio, situated on Italy's west coast, just 30 miles (50 km) from Rome. With the invasion of France imminent, however, troops and landing craft were limited. Costly assaults on the Gustav Line continued, tying down German forces while the Anzio operation unfolded. Shortly before troops landed on January 22, Clark launched a disastrous attack south of Cassino where the Rapido River enters the Liri River. "We had the feeling we were being sacrificed," recalled a sergeant in the U.S. 36th Infantry Division, which lost nearly 1,700 men there.

Fighting intensified at Cassino, linked to Rome by a highway and railroad. Allied forces tried repeatedly to take that town, reduced to rubble by its bombers, which also pulverized the monastery. Monte Cassino remained in enemy hands until it was seized in May by Polish soldiers, who had been released from Soviet prison camps to fight the Germans. Their attack formed part of a huge assault on the Gustav Line, which collapsed shortly before troops at Anzio broke out of the beachhead and advanced on Rome.

FROM ANZIO TO ROME

Two divisions landed unopposed in Operation Shingle at Anzio in January 1944, but their cautious commander, Maj. Gen. John Lucas, did not move out before Germans boxed them in. In February, panzers and infantry penetrated that beachhead. Maj. Gen. Lucian Truscott, commander of the U.S. Third Infantry Division, replaced Lucas at Anzio and awaited reinforcements. In May, he was ordered to cut off the German 10th Army as it retreated. Advancing on May 23, his forces pushed toward Valmontone to block the German retreat. But Fifth Army commander Clark was itching to take Rome and ordered Truscott to divert forces to the capital. Clark's capture of Rome, from which Germans withdrew before his troops arrived on June 5, 1944, was overshadowed by the Allied invasion of Normandy the next day—and by the torturous campaign to liberate northern Italy that continued until the war ended. The demands of the Allied push inland from Normandy meant that troops of the American-led Fifth Army and the British-led Eighth Army fought in Italy without the numerical advantage enjoyed by their comrades elsewhere in Europe. The 20 divisions of those two armies kept 26 German divisions tied down in Italy and broke through the fortified Gothic Line in the mountains north of Florence by December. ■

ABOVE: **This German leaflet designed to demoralize Allied troops shows the beachhead at Anzio**

British and U.S. forces landed in southern Italy in September 1943 and advanced up the boot. Determined German resistance along the Gustav Line south of Rome during the winter of 1943–44 and along the Gothic Line in late 1944 prolonged the war in Italy until Germany surrendered in 1945.

AIR WAR OVER EUROPE

+++++++++++++

In early 1943, Allied leaders approved an Anglo-American bomber offensive in Europe that would blast Axis cities, industries, and strategic targets day and night. The chief of the RAF Bomber Command, Arthur Harris, insisted that pounding German cities at night—when air crews were less vulnerable—was the surest path to victory. Maj. Gen. Ira Eaker, commander of the U.S. Eighth Air Force, believed that airmen in Boeing B-17 Flying Fortresses and Consolidated B-24 Liberators, equipped with machine guns and advanced bombsight, could defend themselves while carrying out precise daytime raids on targets beyond the range of their fighter escorts. But as Eaker noted, the British and Americans could agree to differ by attacking in shifts. "By bombing the devils around the clock," he wrote Churchill, "we can prevent the German defenses from getting any rest."

Eaker learned from bitter experience in 1943 that his planes were highly susceptible to fighter attack when flying without escorts. By 1944, his airmen were being escorted by nimble P-51 Mustang fighters, which when fitted with drop tanks enjoyed an extended range of 2,200 miles (3,500 km).

Both British and American crews bombed cities at night, using incendiaries to kindle firestorms. More than a million Germans were killed or wounded in such attacks, which also cost the lives of many airmen targeted by night fighters and antiaircraft batteries.

LEFT: **An RAF reconnaissance photographer peers through a bulky F24 camera from the open observation port of a bomber in 1940.**

A blackened statue overlooks charred ruins after Allied warplanes fire-bombed Dresden in February 1945, killing nearly 25,000 people.

More effective militarily were air raids on targets like the French railroad network, which was blasted in early 1944 to slow the German response to the looming Allied invasion.

TARGETING THE ENEMY

Aerial reconnaissance, used to gather intelligence on enemy assets and map bombing targets, evolved rapidly during World War II. New cameras had lenses with longer focal lengths and higher resolution for use in reconnaissance aircraft operating above the ceiling of antiaircraft batteries. De Havilland Mosquito reconnaissance planes had a range of more than 2,000 miles (3,200 km) and carried up to four fixed automatic cameras, which could produce stereoscopic images for a three-dimensional view of target areas.

Transforming reconnaissance photographs into targeting maps involved careful research and intelligence analysis. Bombing targets with precision was a greater technological challenge, and civilian fatalities across Europe mounted with every Allied raid.

BOMBING GERMAN CITIES

Beginning in March 1942, RAF heavy bombers blasted German cities with explosives and incendiaries. The first targets chosen by Air Marshal Harris to test incendiary bombing tactics were Lübeck and Rostock on the Baltic whose wooden buildings erupted in flames. In May, Harris launched the first of many "thousand-bomber" raids; in a single night, nearly 500 people died in Cologne.

Targeting industrial centers such as Hamburg—where more than 40,000 people died in a firestorm in July 1943—disrupted German war production, which was soon shifted away from cities. Predictions that strategic bombing would turn civilians against the war proved misguided. Germans gradually lost faith in Hitler, but support for the troops remained firm. Despite repeated bombings of Berlin between August 1943 and March 1944, fewer than 10,000 people were killed there in attacks that cost the RAF more than 2,500 casualties. Blistering assaults on German cities such as Dresden would continue, but the Reich would be defeated not by bombers aloft but by soldiers on the ground. ■

ALLIED BOMBING RAIDS
August – November, 1943
Axis territory, Oct. 7, 1943
Axis satellite or puppet state, Oct. 7, 1943
Allied territory, Oct. 7, 1943
Allied-held territory, Oct. 7, 1943
Neutral state, Oct. 7, 1943
Allied front line
8th Air Force
9th Air Force
15th Air Force
Royal Air Force (RAF)
Airfield and aircraft construction
Densely populated area
Nazi Party center
Oil refinery
Railway center
Secret weapons site
Shipbuilding center
U-boat installation
War industry facility
REICHSKOMMISSARI NORW
North Sea
Edinburgh
Belfast
IRELAND
Dublin
UNITED KINGDOM
Grafton Underwood
Coventry
High Wycombe
Cardiff
Bath
LONDON
Exeter
Dover
200 miles
300 miles
400 miles
500 miles
600 miles
700 miles
800 miles
900 miles
English Channel
REICHSKOMMISSARIAT NETHERLANDS
Wilhelmshaven
Vegesack
Bremen
Amsterdam
Rotterdam
Osnabrück
Essen
Cologne
Dunkirk
Mimoyecques
Lille
Brussels
REICHSKOMMISSARIAT BELGIUM AND N. FRANCE
Koblenz
Frankfurt
Mainz
Abbeville
Martinvast
Sottevast
Périers
Caen
Falaise
Rouen
PARIS
Juvisy-sur-Orge
Saarbrü
Stut
Brest
Lorient
Saint-Nazaire
Loire
Seine
Rhein
Freiburg
Zürich
Bern
SWITZERL
FRANCE
Bay of Biscay
La Pallice
Lyon
Bordeaux
Rhône
Pyrenees
ANDORRA
Marseille
MONA
Ebro
Duero
ATLANTIC OCEAN
PORTUGAL
MADRID
SPAIN
Tagus
Guadiana
Guadalquivir
Lisbon
Barcelona
Corsica (Allied occupied)
Sardinia (Allied occupied)
MED
Strait of Gibraltar
GIBRALTAR (U.K.)
(International Zone) Tangier
Tétouan
SPANISH MOROCCO (Spanish Prot.)
Algiers
Rabat
Casablanca
FRENCH MOROCCO (Allied occupied)
ALGERIA (Allied occupied)

This map shows the range of Allied bombers based in England and Italy, and designates targets including major airfields and railways. The RAF blasted German cities at night, and the U.S. Eighth Air Force conducted daylight raids on strategic targets.
FINLAND
Helsinki
Tallinn
Stockholm
SWEDEN
Riga
Baltic Sea
SOVIET UNION
Soviet front line Oct. 7, 1943
REICHSKOMMISSARIAT OSTLAND
Vilnius
Minsk
Copenhagen
Peenemünde
Rostock
Lübeck
Kharkov (Kharkiv)
Vistula
Warsaw
BERLIN
Braunschweig
Kiev
Magdeburg
Oschersleben
Halberstadt
Rowno (Rivne)
Dnieper
Dnipropetrovs'k
Bernburg
Lützkendorf
Leuna
Dresden
REICHSKOMMISSARIAT UKRAINE
GENERAL GOVERNMENT
Kraków
Prague
TRANSDNIESTRIA
Schweinfurt
Plzeň
PROTECTORATE OF BOHEMIA AND MORAVIA
Nürnberg
Regensburg
Carpathian Mountains
SLOVAKIA
Bratislava
Munich
Linz
VIENNA
HUNGARY
Danube
Budapest
Berchtesgaden
Ploesti (Ploiești)
ROMANIA
Bucharest
Black Sea
Ljubljana
Zagreb
Belgrade
CROATIA
Po
Danube
SAN MARINO
Sarajevo
TERRITORY OF THE MILITARY COMMANDER IN SERBIA
Sofia
ITALY (ITALIAN SOCIAL REPUBLIC)
Adriatic Sea
MONTENEGRO (German occupied)
BULGARIA
Istanbul
United States 15th Air Force begins operations from Foggia Nov. 2, 1943
Cetinje
DALMATIA (German occupied)
Tirana
ROME
Foggia
ALBANIA (German occupied)
TURKEY
Allied front line Oct. 7, 1943
100 miles
GREECE (German military administration, Bulgarian annexation)
Aegean Sea
Tyrrhenian Sea
200 miles
300 miles
Athens
Ionian Sea
Sicily (Allied occ.)
Tunis
Crete
Valletta
MALTA (British Crown Colony)
0 mi 200
0 km 200
October 1943 features are shown.
Present-day city names are in parentheses.

RUSSIA RESURGENT

++++++++++++++

Hitler spent many long hours poring over maps of Russia, but he never fully grasped the enormity of that country or the full extent of the challenges it posed to advancing armies. By late 1941 the Führer's invading forces appeared close to victory, yet a series of punishing Soviet counterattacks penetrated the ground the Germans gained and left many of Hitler's forces stranded as the brutal Russian winter closed in. The Soviets could draw on huge numbers of men and women to defend the homeland, and their armies were remarkably resilient. Stalin's armies proved capable of enduring staggering losses, then striking back.

After his forces failed to reach Moscow and were driven back from the capital in the winter of 1941, Hitler sent armies in pursuit of another distant objective in 1942—oil-rich Baku in the Republic of Azerbaijan across the Caucasus Mountains, a tempting target in a contest that was as much about seizing fuel, food, and other vital resources as it was about seizing Russian territory. The campaign to capture Baku would be carried out by Army Group South, while Army Group Center held firm west of Moscow and Army Group North maintained its grip on Leningrad. Despite bold gains in the region through 1942 and 1943, the drive to Baku faltered in the rugged Caucasus, as the entrenched struggle for Stalingrad and a huge tank collision at Kursk finally pushed the Nazis back toward their own border. By December 1942, the tide had begun to turn in Russia's favor.

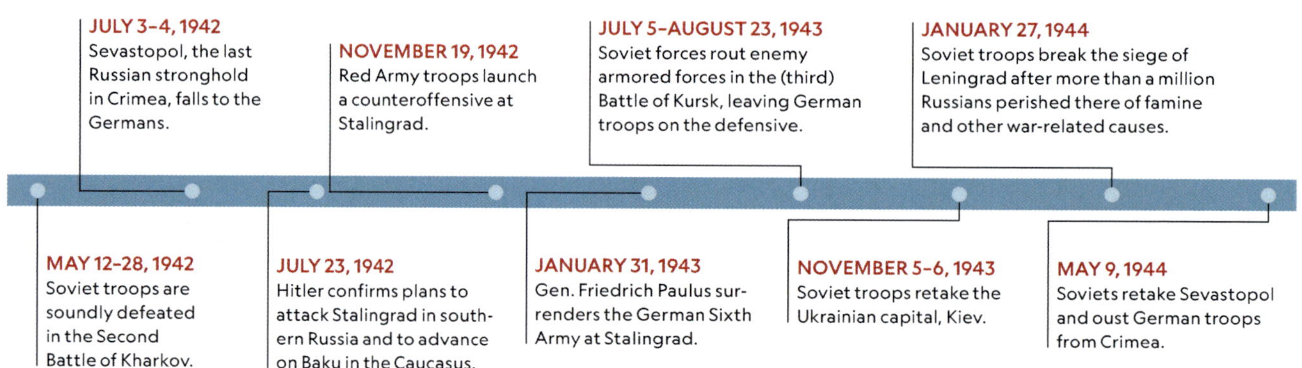

BRUTAL STRUGGLE AT KHARKOV

Unaware that Hitler's Army Group South, led by Field Marshal Fedor von Bock, was being reinforced in the spring of 1942 for its upcoming offensive, Soviet Marshal Semyon Timoshenko prepared to advance against Bock from two salients, or bulges, in the line separating their forces. Timoshenko's objective was to retake Kharkov, Russia's fourth largest city, in a classic pincer movement. Attacking on May 12, Red Army troops in the northern salient made little progress and ground to a halt under Luftwaffe air strikes. But Timoshenko's forces to the south achieved a breakthrough against the Sixth Army, led by Gen. Friedrich Paulus, a staff officer new to field command. As the incursion there deepened, Paulus wanted to pull back his forces but heeded Hitler's order to stand fast while Bock prepared to counterattack.

The counterattack came on May 17 as the First Panzer Army cut behind Timoshenko's troops and bottled them up. Bock's forces squeezed their foes into an ever tighter bind. On May 20, Timoshenko asked his commissar, future Soviet premier Nikita Khrushchev, to persuade Stalin to cancel the offensive and allow troops to break out of their encircled position. Commissars were appointed by the Kremlin to ensure that officers were loyal to the regime and relentless in battling the enemy. Stalin rebuffed Khrushchev and refused to cancel the Kharkov offensive before Timoshenko's troops were doomed. More than 200,000 were captured and 100,000 killed in a disaster that was reminiscent of those suffered by the Red Army in 1941. Timoshenko and Khrushchev feared that Stalin might have them executed. Instead, Stalin demoted Timoshenko and emptied his pipe on Khrushchev's head to humiliate him.

REVISITING STALINGRAD

After this bitter defeat in the Second Battle of Kharkov—the first had occurred when Germans captured the city in October 1941—Stalin allowed commanders to make tactical withdrawals to more defensible positions. Hitler, on the other hand, emerged from the clash

ABOVE: **Russian soldiers fight amid the rubble of Stalingrad, which favored Soviet defenders over German attackers, who had to leave cover to advance.**

TURNING POINT AT STALINGRAD

Hitler's scheme to quickly capture Stalingrad in July 1942 looked feasible on a map, but German troops would have to fight block by block, week after week, until that city became a maze from which there was no escape. Nobody foresaw the terror that would ensue at Stalingrad better than Stalin himself. As German forces approached, the Soviet leader warned that Red Army officers who withdrew would be court-martialed and soldiers who retreated would be shot. During the protracted battle, Russian security forces shot dead more than 13,000 Russian soldiers for cowardice and other offenses.

The vicious street fighting amid the rubble of the city favored Soviet defenders over German attackers, who were forced into the open to advance. "The snipers don't give us any rest," one German officer at Stalingrad wrote. "They shoot bloody well."

Streets, houses, and factories changed hands repeatedly in vicious combat that the Germans called *rattenkrieg* (rat war). Also defending Stalingrad were Russian women who served as medics, snipers, and pilots of the 588th Night Bomber Regiment, who flew planes stitched together from canvas and plywood. Dubbed "Night Witches" by Germans, the unit was heavily decorated for its daring night raids. When the battle ended in February 1943, Stalingrad had become the bloodiest clash of World War II, with some two million men, women, and children killed, wounded, or captured.

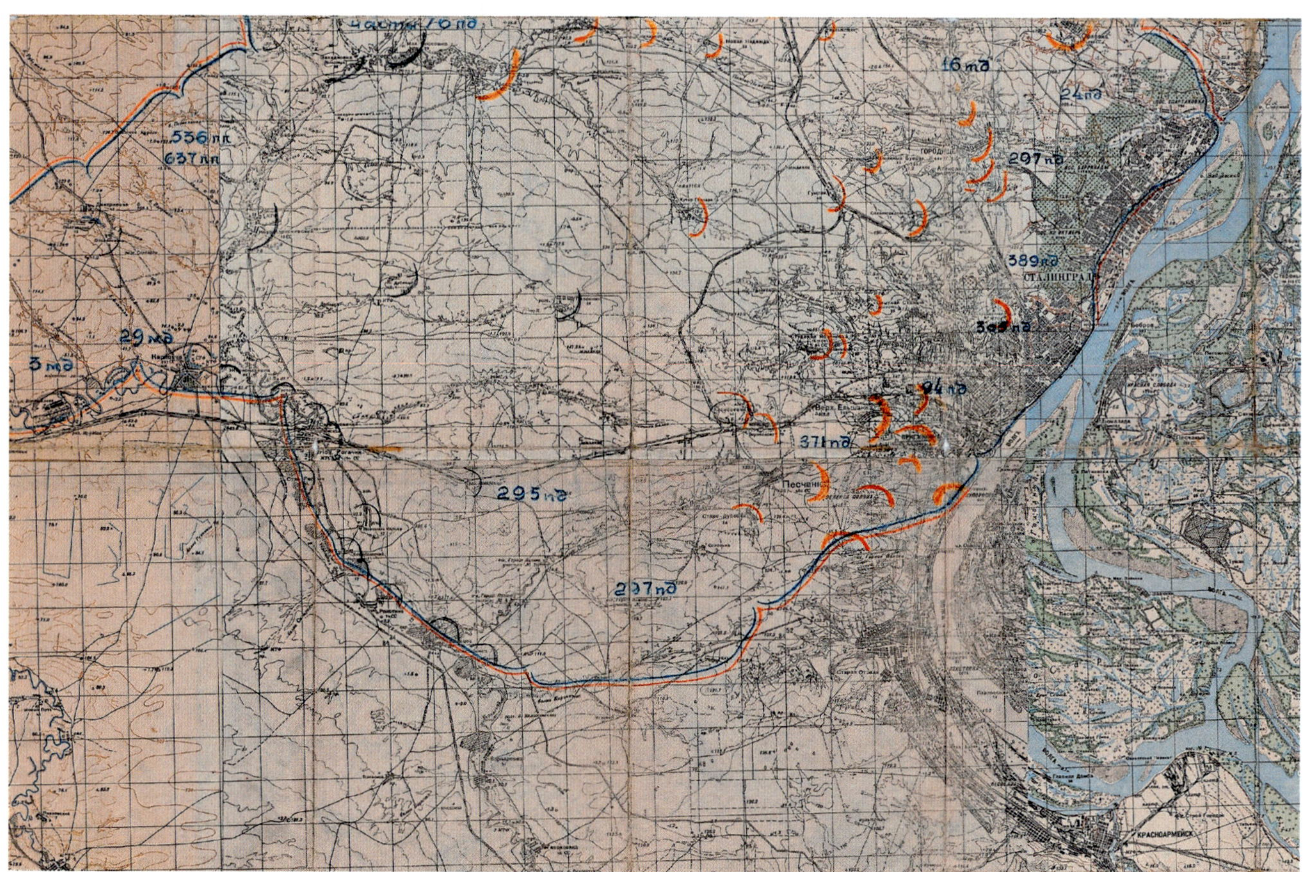

Based on intelligence gathered during the battle, this Russian situation map drawn in early January 1943 shows German units in blue, trapped within the Soviet perimeter west of Stalingrad (outlined in red, with an interior blue line indicating the former German perimeter). Curved orange lines represent Soviet forces, wiping out enemy resistance around Stalingrad. German troops clung desperately to the city but had no way out.

overconfident and spread his troops too thin, sure that Army Group South could both seize Baku and shatter the Voronezh-Stalingrad line. Bock took Voronezh, but Hitler considered him to be too slow and sacked his field marshal in July 1942. He then issued Führer Directive No. 45, which strategized a swift capture of Stalingrad followed by an advance down the Volga River to Astrakhan on the Caspian Sea.

In July, bolstered by the Fourth Panzer Army, General Paulus's 300,000-man-strong Sixth Army pressed Russians into a tight pocket in Stalingrad, with their backs to the Volga. Supplies and reinforcements were ferried to the city from the east bank of the river under heavy fire. In mid-August, the Luftwaffe bombed Stalingrad, killing thousands. But savage street fighting raged on for the next three months, as fierce battles ensued "for every yard of ground, for every brick and stone," as the commander of the Soviet 62nd Army, Gen. Vasily Chuikov, later wrote (see sidebar p. 70).

On November 11, Paulus's German troops made one last push. On November 19, the Red Army launched Operation Uranus, a massive counterattack that overwhelmed Axis troops guarding the German perimeter. Paulus obeyed Hitler's order to stand fast as Soviet pincers closed around the Sixth Army. In early January 1943, Axis forces were surrounded west of Stalingrad. Paulus's men were starving, freezing, and trapped. He surrendered his shattered army, reduced to less than 100,000 men, on January 31. A German commander later called this defeat "the turning point of the entire war."

A CLASH OF TITANS

By the time the Battle of Stalingrad ended, the Germans had been ousted from the Caucasus and relinquished most of the ground they had gained in the summer of 1942. Russian commanders, emboldened by success, pressed ahead in February 1943 and secured much of eastern Ukraine. Russia regained control of Kharkov briefly but Field Marshal Erich von Manstein, a keen

ABOVE: **Russian soldiers fought desperately against German invaders during the Second Battle of Kharkov in May 1942.**

German strategist, recognized that the Russians were overextended and recaptured Kharkov in March, leaving Soviet troops in a salient that encompassed Kursk. Operation Citadel, the German plan to cut off that salient and regain Kursk, took several months to develop. Cautious after the disaster at Stalingrad, Hitler agreed to delay action until heavier German tanks could be sent to the battlefront. Warned of the attack by spies, the Soviets prepared to thwart enemy onslaughts with tank traps, minefields, artillery, Katyusha rockets, and air strikes before committing the bulk of their armor to battle.

The Battle of Kursk began at dawn on July 5, when Gen. Hermann Hoth's Fourth Panzer Army, heavily reinforced after Stalingrad, pushed into the salient from the south while Gen. Walther Model's Ninth Army, replete with panzer divisions, advanced from the north. Altogether, the Germans threw 900,000 troops and 2,700 tanks into the conflict. Awaiting them were more than a million Soviets, 3,600 tanks, and the strongest anti-tank defenses the Germans had ever encountered. Both sides preceded massive armored assaults with air strikes, with warplanes streaking ahead of tanks to bomb enemy forces. Over the course of five grueling days, Hoth's panzers advanced just 20 miles (32 km) and Model's forces managed only eight miles (13 km). Prospects that the two armies would meet as planned and surround their foes faded fast. After a head-on clash near Prokhorovka on July 12 in which Hoth's forces destroyed many more tanks than they lost but gained little ground, Soviets counterattacked and Hitler was forced to scrub Operation Citadel and cede Kursk back to the Russians.

GERMANS IN RETREAT

Gen. Ivan Konev, whose tanks and troops helped contain Hoth's panzers, called the Battle of Kursk the "swan song of the German armored force," which had shredded Russian lines in the past. After defeating their foes at Kursk, Soviet troops made rapid gains in Ukraine, recapturing Kiev in November 1943. An invasion that Hitler thought would smash the Soviet state in a few months had now consumed two years. Every gain Hitler made with his awesome armored divisions had been negated by the sheer numbers of the resisting Soviet forces or by the vast distances of the Russian realm he sought to conquer. Within the next 12 months, the Soviets would finally break the long siege of Leningrad, retake Sevastopol in Crimea, and liberate their homeland from German invaders, who would leave behind nearly two million men dead or captured. The larger question was no longer whether the Soviet Union would survive the Nazi invasion but whether Nazi Germany could avoid destruction as Stalin's vengeful armies chased it back to Berlin. ■

LEFT: **Warplanes streak ahead of Russian tanks to bomb German forces during the Battle of Kursk.**

THE FINAL SOLUTION

In January 1942, SS security chief Reinhard Heydrich announced the "Final Solution of the Jewish Question," or extermination by gas chambers. Many of the six million Jewish men, women, and children who perished in the Holocaust were killed in extermination camps, but some were sent to forced labor camps. They were joined by Romany, Jehovah's Witnesses, Communists, dissidents, prisoners of war, homosexuals, and captured Allied agents.

In a futile effort to eliminate evidence, SS chief Heinrich Himmler ordered some camps evacuated and dismantled as Soviet troops approached in 1945. Prisoners were often marched to camps farther from Allied lines, and many died along the way. The horrors of the Nazi regime were laid bare when Allied troops liberated camps whose guards had fled, leaving behind bones in crematoriums and skeletal prisoners. Such appalling evidence of genocide raised a troubling question: What could the Allies have done to combat the systematic murder of millions? In mid-1944, the U.S. War Department had considered proposals to bomb Auschwitz, a killing center where as many as 10,000 people a day died in gas chambers. Authorities decided against it, mainly to avoid diverting resources from attacks on other pressing targets in Germany. But they also wanted to avoid killing prisoners. It was hard to map targets, and even harder to bomb precise structures like gas chambers without destroying nearby barracks housing tens of thousands of innocent inmates.

Rail lines transported victims to extermination camps established by the SS in Germany and its puppet states.

Troops of the U.S. First Infantry Division wade ashore under fire at Omaha Beach on D-Day, June 6, 1944.

CHAPTER 4

VICTORY IN EUROPE

1944-1945

By gaining supremacy in the Atlantic in 1943, the Allies facilitated a huge buildup of American troops and equipment in Britain. Between January and June 1944, 800,000 soldiers crossed the Atlantic to bolster the long-anticipated invasion of German-occupied France, designated Operation Overlord. Allied pilots blasted French railways and bridges to stop their foes from rushing reserves to Normandy. Battle-tested Anglo-American commanders, including Eisenhower, Patton, and Montgomery, prepared to lead troops against Germany's Erwin Rommel, who was assigned to the French coastal defenses while most of the German Army tried to repel the Soviets on the Eastern Front.

The Allied invasion began in the early hours of June 6, 1944. Although the landings were less costly than feared, American forces paid a dreadful price before securing Omaha Beach. Casualties mounted as invasion forces advanced inland. Not until late July did they break out of the beachhead. On August 15, a second invasion, Operation Anvil, unfolded on the French Mediterranean coast. Allied troops liberated Paris in late August.

On the Eastern Front, the Red Army captured Poland before invading Germany through East Prussia. The advance of Western Allies had stalled at the West Wall (Siegfried Line) along the German border. The Battle of the Bulge in January 1945 delayed their advance across the Rhine until March while vengeful Soviets closed in on Berlin. "We may be destroyed," Hitler had remarked earlier, "but if we are, we shall drag a world with us—a world in flames." On April 30, with Berlin about to fall to the Russians, Hitler committed suicide. A week later, Germany surrendered.

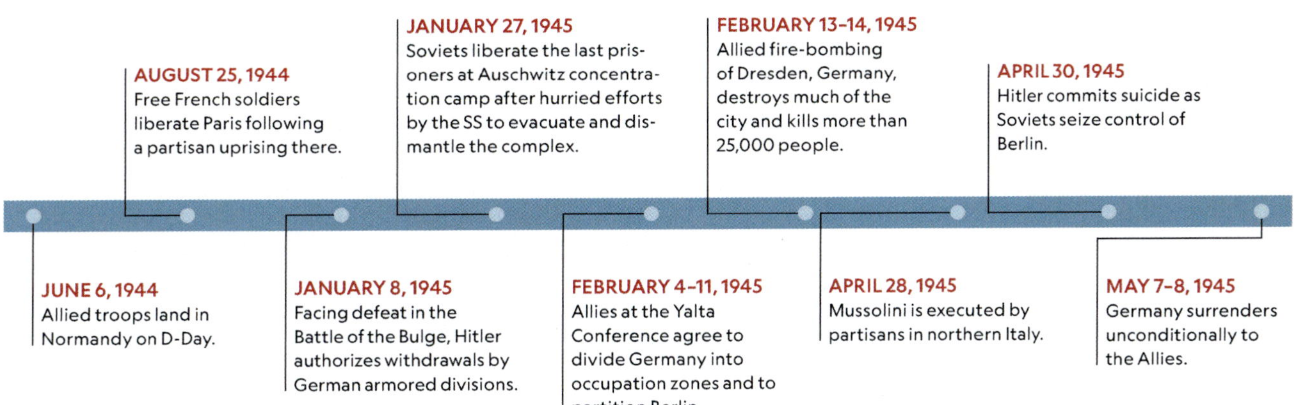

INVASION OF NORMANDY

++++++++++++

Planning for Operation Overlord began in London more than a year in advance. Allied staff officers led by Lt. Gen. Frederick Morgan debated where to pierce the Atlantic Wall, the German coastal fortifications that extended from Norway to the southwest coast of France. The shortest route to Germany lay across the Strait of Dover, but the Atlantic Wall was at its strongest at Calais. Morgan and staff decided on the coast of Normandy, which lay farther from Germany but was less heavily fortified. Their original plan (recorded in the top secret documents at right) called for three divisions to land on a narrow front on D-Day. But when Eisenhower and Montgomery arrived in London in early 1944 to serve respectively as supreme commander and field commander of the Allied Expeditionary Force, they altered the plan based on amphibious operations in Italy. Five divisions would land on D-Day on a broader front, supported by three airborne divisions and followed by an immense influx of men and materiel. A second invasion of France along the Mediterranean coast would take place a few months later.

> WE'LL HAVE ONLY ONE CHANCE TO STOP THE ENEMY, AND THAT'S WHILE HE'S IN THE WATER... STRUGGLING TO GET ASHORE.
>
> —GEN. ERWIN ROMMEL

German commanders did not ignore the potential threat to Normandy. Rommel—in charge of Army Group B under Field Marshal Gerd von Rundstedt, German commander in chief in the West—laced beaches there with mines and obstructions to force landing craft to disgorge troops at low tide, leaving them more exposed. Rommel wanted panzer divisions deployed in Normandy to repulse invaders before they established a beachhead. "Everything we have must be on the coast," he insisted. Rundstedt disagreed, and Hitler decided to hold most German armored forces in reserve until the invasion took place. Only one panzer division guarded the Normandy coast. An elaborate Allied deception campaign called Operation Bodyguard—which included simulating

OPPOSITE: **Rommel inspects a beach near Calais in April 1944, checking obstacles laid to snag landing craft and amphibious tanks.**

THE D-DAY DECEPTION

Operation Overlord was shielded from the Germans by the fabricated Operation Bodyguard, inspired by Churchill's remark that truth in wartime should always be "attended by a bodyguard of lies." That meant simulating preparations for landings elsewhere than Normandy to keep German forces dispersed. Bodyguard deceptions fed Hitler's fears of invasions across much of occupied Europe, from Norway to Greece. But the Germans viewed an invasion across the Strait of Dover as most likely—an expectation that Allied intelligence officers helped reinforce.

While planners for Overlord produced detailed maps of the Normandy landing zone for Montgomery's 21st Army Group, the masterminds of Bodyguard concocted a fictional invasion force called FUSAG (First U.S. Army Group), supposedly consisting of 50 divisions preparing to cross the Strait of Dover after Montgomery's diversionary landing at Normandy. General Patton played the part of FUSAG's commander by conspicuously reviewing a few real units assigned to him. Props for the hoax included dummy tanks and warplanes that would look convincing to German reconnaissance pilots flying over Dover, where Patton's legions were reportedly massing. The cunning double agent Juan Pujol Garcia, who had enlisted as a German spy with the intention of serving the Allies, filed false reports that helped keep German troops tied down at Calais awaiting the fictitious army group long after Overlord unfolded.

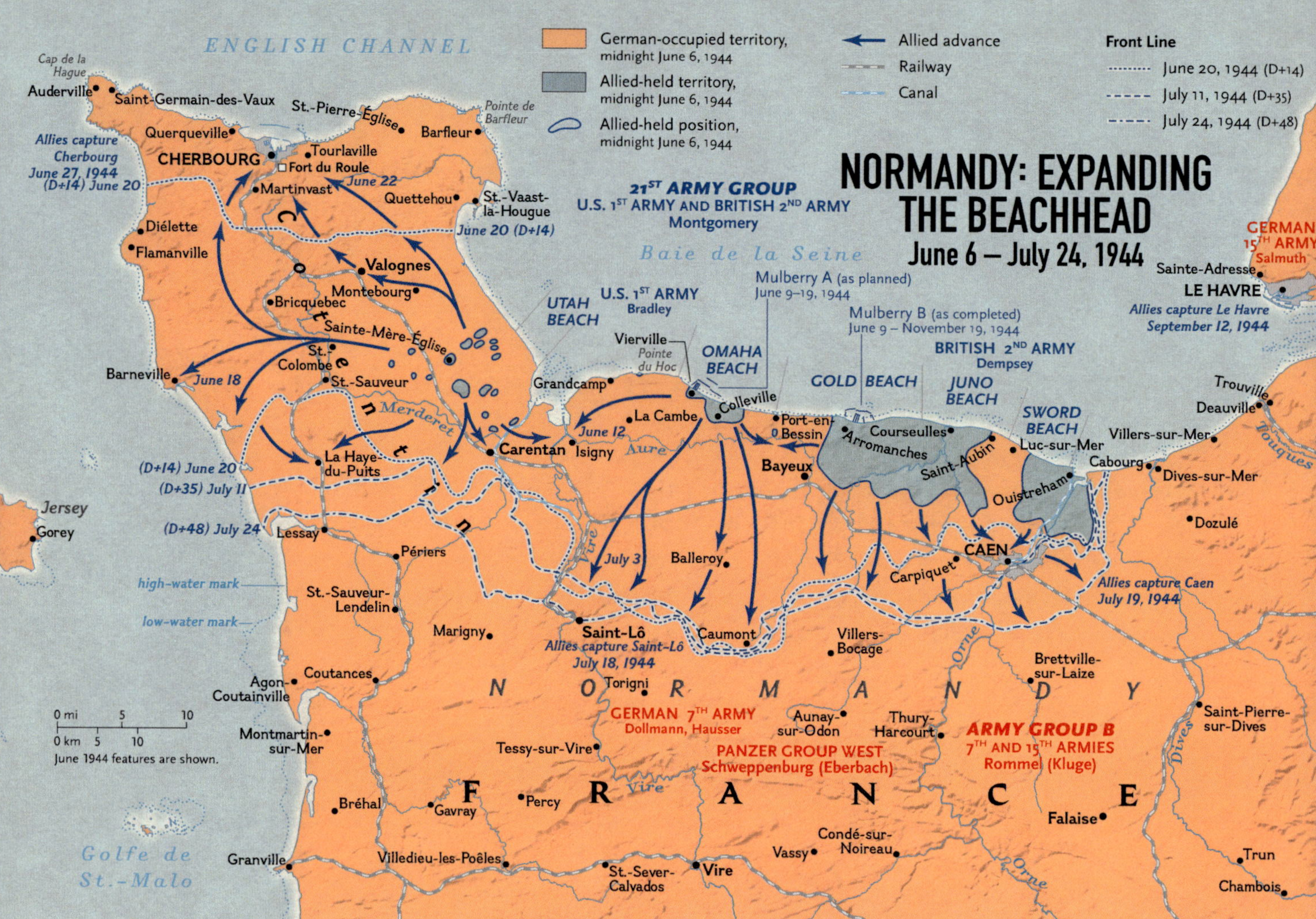

The Allies made fitful progress in expanding the beachhead in Normandy from D-Day to July 24. To the west, troops of the U.S. First Army—led by Omar Bradley—fought their way in June up the Cotentin Peninsula to Cherbourg. To the east, British and Canadian forces of Montgomery's 21st Army Group met with stiff opposition from German panzer divisions around Caen.

phantom divisions and feeding false reports to Berlin from German agents under British control—led Hitler to view landings at Normandy as a diversion, which would be followed by a massive Allied thrust across the Strait of Dover.

LANDING UNDER FIRE

Foul weather forced Eisenhower to postpone Overlord until June 6, after which two weeks would pass before the moon and tides were again favorable for paratroopers landing inland before dawn and soldiers landing on the beaches at daybreak. His decision to proceed on the 6th, during a lull in the storm, caught German commanders by surprise. But some Allied landing craft and amphibious tanks sank in swells, and many men were seasick. Nausea mingled with dread as they disembarked under fire. "Many were hit in the water and drowned," recalled Sgt. Bob Slaughter of the U.S. 29th Infantry Regiment. "There were dead men in the water and live men acting dead, letting the tide take them in."

Nearly 3,000 Americans were killed or wounded on Omaha Beach. As shell fire from Allied warships began silencing enemy gunners on the cliffs, soldiers rallied and pushed inland toward Colleville-sur-Mer. Americans who landed at Utah Beach faced little resistance, and British and Canadian troops advanced several miles inland and withstood a late-day counterattack by the 21st Panzer Division. When Rommel returned that night

OPPOSITE: **American soldiers like these gunners firing an M3 105-mm light howitzer encountered fierce resistance as they pushed south from Carentan, below Utah Beach.**

to Normandy, his worst fears were realized. He had warned a fellow officer that their only chance was to stop the enemy in the water. Now nearly 160,000 Allied troops had landed.

EXPANDING THE BEACHHEAD

Following D-Day, the Allies had to transport troops and supplies to Normandy without access to a deepwater port. Germans assumed that their foes would require such a port, which lent credence to Allied deceptions portraying the Normandy landings as a diversion, to be followed by a big push aimed at a port like Calais. While the German 15th Army guarded Calais, the Allies reinforced their Normandy beachhead by constructing artificial harbors called mulberries, using components prefabricated in British ports and towed across the English Channel. Mulberry A, completed off Omaha Beach in mid-June and linked to shore by a pontoon bridge, was wrecked a few days later by a fierce storm. Mulberry B, constructed off Gold Beach near Arromanches, withstood that storm and helped boost Allied strength in Normandy to a million men by early July.

Reinforcements for the troops who landed on D-Day were essential because expanding the beachhead proved difficult. Inland from the beaches lay the forbidding bocage terrain, consisting of low fields surrounded by dense hedgerows that sheltered German snipers, machine-gunners, and anti-tank units. Not until June 27 did American troops seize the deepwater port of Cherbourg, which German retreating forces damaged extensively. Another important objective, heavily defended Caen, was not taken on D-Day, as Montgomery planned, and held out against repeated attacks. On June 13, the British Seventh Armored Division tried to outflank Caen but was repulsed at Villers-Bocage by elements of the First and Second SS Panzer Divisions. Allied bombers blasted Caen on July 6, killing many French civilians but few Germans, who withdrew south of the city and resisted tenaciously as Montgomery tried to punch through their defenses. Although held in check, his forces kept several German armored divisions tied down while American troops prepared to launch Operation Cobra at Saint-Lô, west of Caen, and break out of the beachhead.

ALLIED BREAKOUT

+++++++++++++

On July 25, 1944, more than 1,500 B-17 and B-24 long-range heavy bombers launched the Allies' Operation Cobra by carpet bombing German lines near Saint-Lô, France. Beyond these lines the tangled bocage terrain gave way to clearer country allowing for more open warfare and rapid advances. Some bombs went astray, killing American troops. But the attack devastated enemy units like the Panzer Lehr Division, led by Gen. Fritz Bayerlein. "My front lines looked like the face of the moon," he ruefully related, "and at least 70 percent of my troops were knocked out—dead, wounded, crazed or numbed." His once dreaded division was left with only 14 tanks: "We could do nothing but retreat."

Among the American forces that poured through gaps forged by the bombers was Patton's newly arrived Third Army. No longer posing as commander of a fictional army group destined for Calais, Patton served now under Omar Bradley, who on August 1 took charge of the genuine 12th Army Group, including the First Army, which he entrusted to Lt. Gen. Courtney Hodges. As Bradley's forces advanced southward into Brittany, Hitler tried to cut them off by ordering a reckless counterattack from battered divisions of the German Seventh Army at Mortain, where the panzers were blasted by artillery and air strikes. Patton then mounted his own version of blitzkrieg by sending armored divisions sweeping around the southern flank of the German Seventh Army while Montgomery's forces advanced to the north against the depleted Fifth Panzer Army. Caught in a pocket at Falaise, at least 50,000 Germans were killed, wounded, or captured. But many escaped

LEFT: **A dazed Canadian soldier of Montgomery's 21st Army Group is treated by a medic near a burning German tank during the push inland toward Caen.**

when Field Marshal Günther von Kluge—who had taken charge of all German forces in France after Rundstedt was relieved and Rommel was wounded—allowed units to retreat without Hitler's permission.

Back in Germany, an internal assassination plot was unfolding against the Führer. Both Rommel and Kluge learned of the plot in advance but chose not to warn Hitler. On July 20, a bomb exploded at the Führer's headquarters but did not kill him. Recalled by Hitler to Germany in August, Kluge took his own life, as Rommel would two months later. In a letter written before he died, Kluge urged Hitler to spare Germans further suffering by ending "a struggle which has become hopeless." But Hitler would not surrender. The Allies who had finally broken out in France would now have to batter their way into Germany.

OPERATION DRAGOON

Originally designated Operation Anvil and planned to coincide with the invasion of Normandy, the Allied invasion of southern France was renamed Operation Dragoon and postponed until August 1944. By then, many German troops in the south had been shifted northward to defend against the onslaught in Normandy. Those who remained behind were left vulnerable to attack. Objectives for Allied forces assigned to Dragoon included capturing Marseille and other ports on the Mediterranean where supplies and reinforcements could be delivered, cutting off enemy forces in the south, and linking up with Allied armies in northern France for the decisive invasion of Germany.

Before dawn on August 15, American and British paratroopers of the First Airborne Task Force began landing inland to secure high ground along the French Riviera, where Gen. Lucian Truscott's U.S. VI Corps, transferred from Italy, came ashore at daybreak. Gains by Truscott's men and by Free French troops—who secured the ports of Marseille and Toulon—forced the German 19th Army to withdraw northward along the Rhône River. Truscott's

ABOVE: **Allied paratroopers descend near the French Riviera on August 15, 1944, to join Operation Dragoon.**

corps then moved to cut off the Germans in the vicinity of Montélimar but met with strong resistance. Although much of the 19th Army escaped, more than 50,000 Germans were captured or killed before they could squeeze through the gap that VI Corps closed in late August. As one witness reported, Allied air strikes on roads clogged with German vehicles left "an inextricable tangle of twisted steel frames and charred corpses," which only bulldozers could clear.

Within three weeks of landing on France's Mediterranean coast, Allied troops aided by French partisans had liberated much of southern France and linked up with invasion forces advancing eastward from Normandy. Operation Dragoon—undertaken over the objection of Churchill, who argued instead for an advance from Italy into the Balkans—strengthened Eisenhower's bid to invade Germany through France, which he and U.S. Army chief George Marshall had long viewed as the one sure path to victory.

> PARIS MUST NOT FALL INTO THE HANDS OF THE ENEMY EXCEPT AS A FIELD OF RUINS.
>
> —ADOLF HITLER

THE LIBERATION OF PARIS

Parisians did not wait for Allied troops to free their city. On August 19, a loose coalition of resistance fighters known as French Forces of the Interior (FFI), which

BELOW: **On August 19, French forces entered Paris in triumph. Americans who followed were hailed as heroes, like these troops of the 28th Infantry Division, shown parading down the Champs-Élysées on August 29.**

included Communists as well as followers of Free French leader Charles de Gaulle, rose up against German occupation forces in Paris. German commander Gen. Dietrich von Choltitz had orders from Hitler to destroy the city rather than surrender it. "Paris must not fall into the hands of the enemy," Hitler insisted, "except as a field of ruins." Reluctant to take actions that might brand him as a war criminal, Choltitz arranged a truce with the FFI that soon collapsed. "As long as there is a single German left in Paris, we shall fight," declared Henri Rol-Tanguy, a Communist firebrand known as Colonel Rol. Concerned that the uprising might fail and subject Parisians to reprisals—or succeed and leave Communists in control—de Gaulle urged Eisenhower to send in Allied troops, led by the French Second Armored Division.

French forces broke through German defenses outside Paris, where partisans had manned the barricades since an uprising began on August 19. When the French troops entered the city on August 25, Choltitz defied orders and surrendered. On August 29, men of the U.S. 28th Infantry Division marched in a victory parade through Paris that took them down the Champs-Élysées within sight of Napoleon's Arc de Triomphe. They then went straight to the front north of the city to resume the war against Germany, which Hitler would prolong until Berlin lay in ruins.

FRENCH RESISTANCE

Before and after D-Day, Allied agents of the U.S. Office of Strategic Services (OSS), its British counterpart the Special Operations Executive (SOE), and the Free French government-in-exile armed covert resistance groups operating within French borders and organized attacks that hindered German opposition to the invasion of Normandy. Among those agents was American-born Virginia Hall, who had aided resistance groups in France for the SOE before fleeing to Spain in late 1942 to evade the Gestapo, whose officers knew she had a conspicuous wooden leg. In early 1944, she transferred to the OSS, dyed her hair gray, and returned furtively to France disguised as a lame old peasant woman to arrange airdrops of weapons to French guerrillas known as the Maquis. She communicated by radio of the type supplied to Allied agents (shown at right)—a perilous assignment because Germans monitored radio transmissions and could trace them to their source. Although the Gestapo was on the lookout for Hall and considered her "one of the most dangerous Allied agents in France," she avoided arrest and linked up after D-Day with one of the many Jedburgh teams, consisting of OSS, SOE, and Free French operatives who parachuted behind enemy lines to coordinate partisan assaults on German troops and their lines of communication.

Like the Allied agents who aided them, French partisans defied German forces at great risk. On June 10, troops of the Second SS Panzer Division ("Das Reich"), which was redeployed from southern France to Normandy after D-Day, retaliated for delaying ambushes by slaughtering inhabitants of the small town of Oradour-sur-Glane. Among the victims were more than 400 women and children, locked in a church that was set aflame. Expected to reach Normandy within a few days, that SS division did not arrive there for a few weeks, too late to repulse the invasion.

PURSUIT TO THE WEST WALL

+++++++++++++

After liberating Paris, the Allied advance eastward to Berlin first had to pass through German-occupied Belgium and Holland. A new theater of ground war, with supply lines secured from Britain and the U.S., had to be established in Western Europe before the continent could be wrenched from Hitler's grip. In September 1944, Montgomery's 21st Army Group seized the Belgian port of Antwerp. Fuel and supplies could not be delivered there, however, until the Allies seized German batteries along the Schelde River. Montgomery proposed to leap ahead by sending paratroopers to seize bridges in Holland that his forces could use to cross the Rhine River and invade the Ruhr, Germany's industrial heartland (see map opposite). Designated Market Garden, the operation collapsed in late September at Arnhem when German forces prevented the Allies from seizing a crucial bridge.

Antwerp did not begin receiving supplies until late November. That slowed advances by Bradley's 12th Army Group, including Patton's Third Army, which ran short of fuel as it approached the West Wall (Siegfried Line), Germany's defensive western barrier. "My men can eat their belts," Patton said, "but my tanks have gotta have gas." The one significant breach in the West Wall that autumn was achieved largely by the battle-tested U.S. First Infantry Division who combined with the U.S. 30th to seize the German city of Aachen. But Eisenhower lacked resources to exploit that breakthrough.

> MY MEN CAN EAT THEIR BELTS, BUT MY TANKS HAVE GOTTA HAVE GAS.
>
> —GENERAL PATTON, ALLIED SUPREME COMMANDER IN WESTERN EUROPE

BATTLE OF THE BULGE

In late 1944, Soviet troops entered East Prussia but Hitler chose to commit German reserves on the Western Front. By enlisting all able-bodied males between 16 and 60, he created new Volksgrenadier divisions and replenished depleted units for an assault on American lines in the forested Ardennes. Hitler's aim was to recapture Antwerp and stall Allied armies in the West.

Launched on December 16, the attack caught Americans in the snow-covered Ardennes by surprise and pushed them back, forming a bulge in the front that

Allied paratroopers flew from England (map above) and dropped behind enemy lines during the failed Operation Market Garden. U.S. paratroopers seized some bridges, but others were foiled by German units who also kept British tanks from reaching Arnhem, where SS panzer divisions crushed the British First Airborne (map left).

would soon be 50 miles (80 km) deep (see maps opposite). Bad weather prevented the Allies from launching air strikes or landing paratroopers, but Eisenhower sent 11,000 men of the 101st Airborne Division in trucks to hold Bastogne, a vital crossroads. Brig. Gen. Anthony McAuliffe's men kept up the fight until tanks of Patton's Fourth Armored Division broke through on December 26 and secured Bastogne. The bulge became a death trap for thousands of Germans, exposed to air strikes as the skies cleared. Hitler's decision to commit the Luftwaffe to the battle on January 1, 1945, failed to avert a bitter defeat. All he achieved was to delay an Allied push into Germany that would prove relatively merciful for civilians, while Soviet troops, hell-bent on revenge, advanced toward Berlin from the east.

ACROSS THE RHINE

After winning the Battle of the Bulge, Allied forces under Eisenhower prepared to storm Germany by piercing the West Wall and crossing the broad Rhine River. A three-prong attack was planned: Montgomery's forces advancing toward the Rhine from central Holland; the U.S. Ninth Army crossing the Rur River in southern Holland; and Bradley's American forces advancing to the south.

Montgomery's forces met with stiff resistance on February 8 near Nijmegen. The Germans destroyed dams on the Rur River, causing floods that stalled the Ninth Army for two weeks. By late February, however, both the U.S. Ninth Army and the First Army were pushing the enemy back toward the Rhine. Germans withdrew across the river, destroying bridges behind them. On March 7, the Allies finally crossed the Rhine threshold: A railroad bridge at Remagen was captured and American

ABOVE: **In October 1944, the defense of Aachen included these 155-mm guns mounted on the chassis of Sherman tanks, which targeted the U.S. First and 30th Infantry Divisions that had crossed into Germany.**

engineers were able to lay pontoon bridges across the river for the advancing First Army troops.

In late March, the Allies launched their major push across the Rhine. By March 30, pincers consisting of Montgomery's forces to the north and Bradley's forces to the south were closing around Field Marshal Walther Model's depleted Army Group B in the Ruhr. Deemed a war criminal by the Soviets for his brutal campaigns in Russia that did not spare citizens, Model took his own life when his forces were surrounded in April.

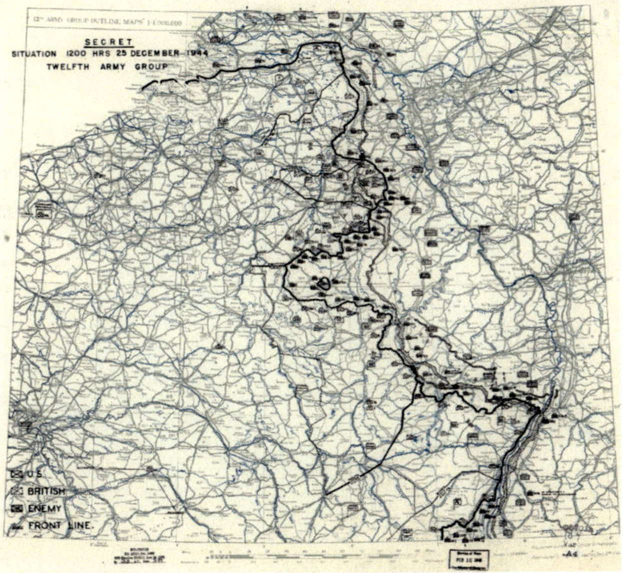

December 25

January 1

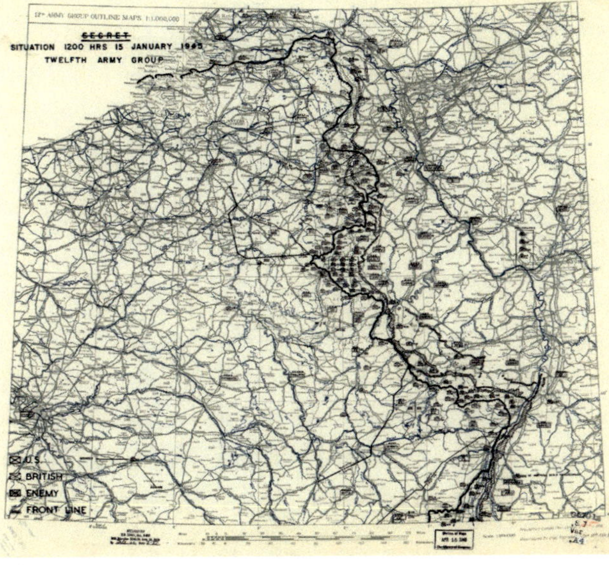

January 15

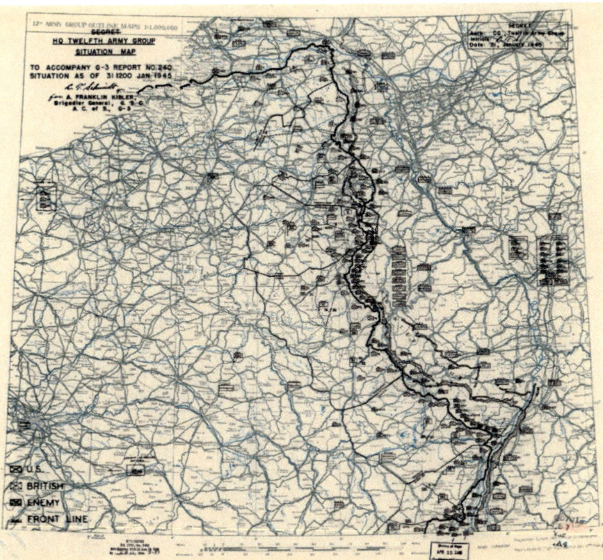

January 31

The Battle of the Bulge is charted in this series of four situation maps. On December 25, 1944 (top left), the 101st Airborne Division was surrounded at Bastogne, amid the bulge, but Patton's Fourth Armored Division was approaching from the south and reached Bastogne the next day. By January 1, 1945 (top right), the bulge was deeper as some Germans had advanced west toward the Meuse River. But it was also narrower because the 101st Airborne and other American units had pushed north from Bastogne, placing German units to the west at risk of encirclement. By January 15 (below left), Hitler had authorized withdrawals and the bulge had receded. By January 31 (below right), Allied troops had closed off the bulge and won the battle.

THE RED ARMY'S ADVANCE

+++++++++++++

On June 22, 1944, three years to the day after German troops invaded Soviet territory, the Red Army launched Operation Bagration, a massive offensive on the Eastern Front aimed primarily at annihilating Army Group Center, the once mighty force that reached the outskirts of Moscow in 1941. Having since recaptured from the Germans nearly all the ground the Soviet Union held before the war began, the Red Army now advanced into areas that Stalin had annexed following his ill-fated pact with Hitler in 1939, including the Baltic states and Belarus, a borderland long disputed by Russia and Poland. Deceptions indicating a Russian offensive to the south around the Black Sea left Germans to the north exposed when nearly 1.5 million Soviet troops attacked. Hitler made things worse by not allowing forces caught in that onslaught to withdraw until it was too late. The Fourth and Ninth Armies were decimated as pincers closed around them at Minsk, and the Third Panzer Army was hard hit as well. Russians then advanced into German-annexed Poland before halting to regroup in August at the Vistula River near Warsaw, where a determined uprising by Polish partisans against German occupation forces was eventually crushed. This was an attempt to oust the Germans and seize control of the city before the advancing Soviets occupied it. The Russians urged the Polish partisans to revolt, but then refused to send support, as promised. The surrender of Poland's Home Army in October allowed the pro-Soviet Polish administration, rather than the

LEFT: **American soldiers embrace their Russian counterparts on entering the Soviet occupation zone in late April 1945.**

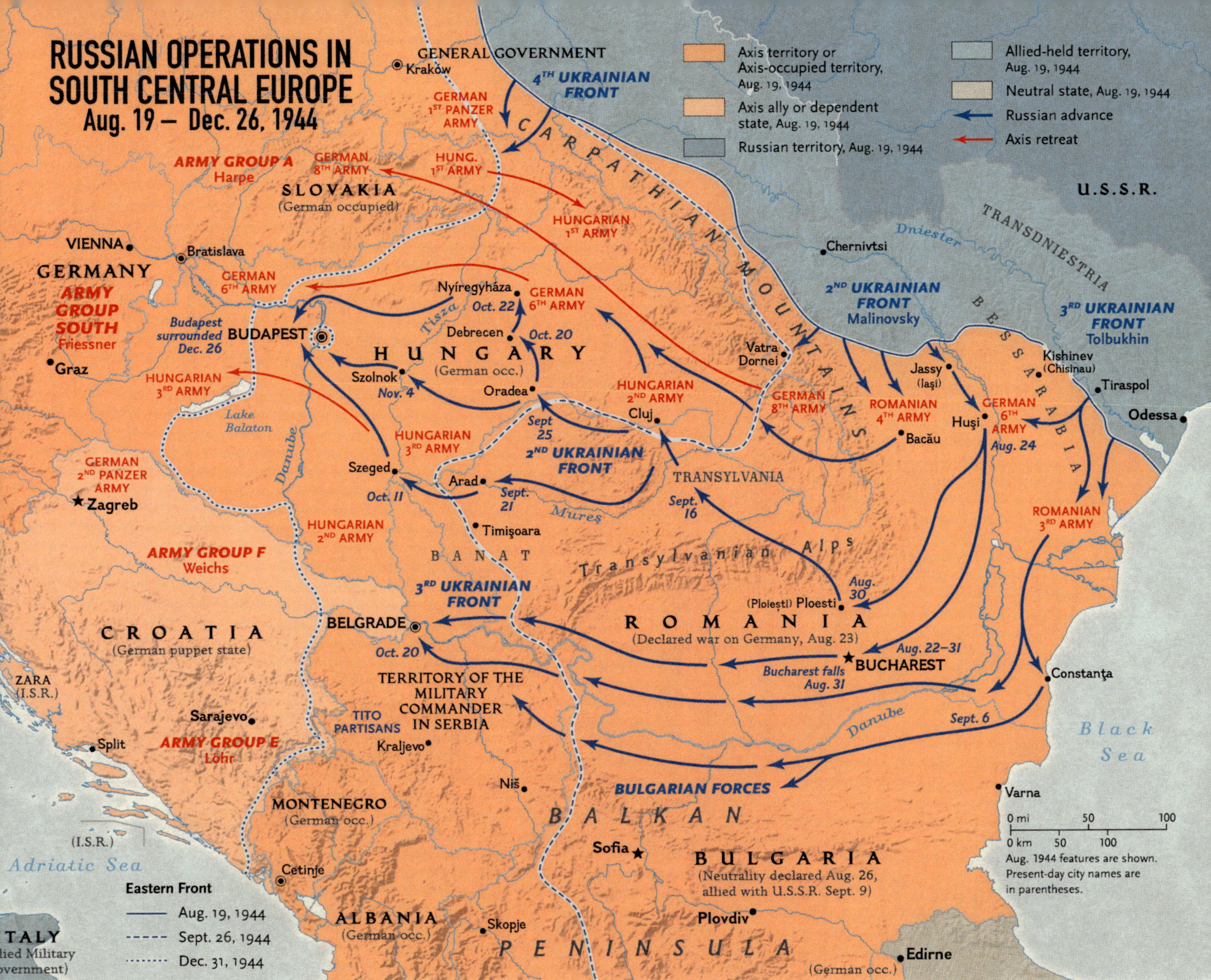

An offensive launched in August 1944 brought Romania, Bulgaria, and Hungary under Soviet control. Russians also entered territory that would soon be reconstituted as Yugoslavia by Marshal Tito, a Communist who would resist alignment with Moscow.

Polish government-in-exile in London, to gain control of the country.

The Red Army did not renew its offensive in Poland and take Warsaw until January 1945. In the meantime, Russian troops made great strides to the north—where they advanced from the Baltic states into East Prussia—and momentous gains to the south, where they invaded Romania and other nations allied with Germany (see map above). After Soviets seized the Ploesti oilfields and denied their output to fuel-hungry German forces, King Michael I of Romania ousted that country's pro-Nazi dictator, Ion Antonescu, and yielded to Russia. Bulgaria switched sides as well, but German troops kept Hungary from leaving the Axis until Budapest fell in February 1945. By then, the Soviets were poised to deliver the deathblow to Hitler's regime in Berlin—and to dominate Eastern Europe behind the "Iron Curtain" for decades to come. Winston Churchill would observe of postwar, Soviet-influenced Eastern Europe, "From Stettin in the Baltic to Trieste in the Adriatic, an iron curtain has descended across the Continent."

THE FALL OF BERLIN

The final battle in the savage struggle between Germany and Russia opened before dawn on April 16, 1945, when Soviet artillery along the Oder River unleashed a thunderous bombardment that reverberated 40 miles (65 km) away on the outskirts of Berlin. German troops

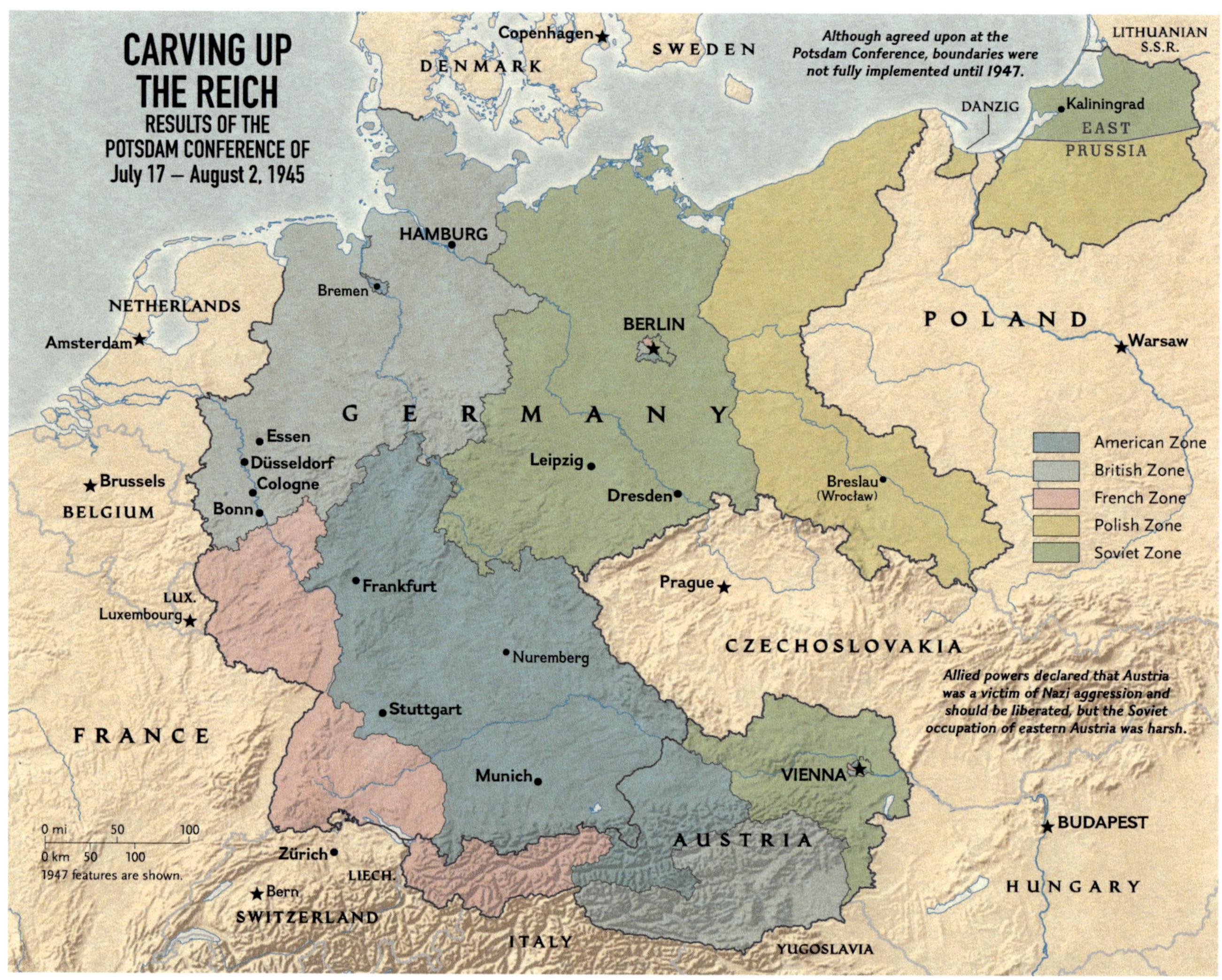

This map shows postwar Soviet, American, British, French, and Polish occupation zones in Germany and Austria. The partition was not confirmed until Allied leaders met at Potsdam in July 1945. Nothing prohibited U.S. forces from entering the proposed Soviet zone in April 1945 and seizing Berlin, as urged by Churchill, but Eisenhower decided to concentrate on securing western Germany.

CARVING UP THE REICH

When Stalin met Roosevelt and Churchill at the Yalta Conference in February 1945, the Red Army occupied eastern Germany while American, British, and French troops occupied western Germany. Separate occupation zones were drawn up along with plans to divide Berlin among the Allies.

After Eisenhower's troops seized the Ruhr region in April, opposition wilted in western Germany but persisted in the east, as Russian soldiers enraged by the brutal occupation of their homeland raped German women and committed other atrocities. Millions fled westward to escape the Soviets. American units entered the Soviet zone and met Russian forces along the Elbe and Mulde Rivers. Churchill had urged Eisenhower to take Berlin but the Americans stopped short. Commander Omar Bradley estimated that seizing the capital would cost at least 100,000 casualties, calling that a "pretty stiff price to pay for a prestige objective . . . especially when we've got to fall back and let the other fellow take over." Soviet commanders were eager to storm Berlin and annihilate Hitler's Reich.

had pulled back to avoid that pounding and held firm initially. But they could not long withstand onslaughts by the First Belorussian Front under Marshal Georgi Zhukov, hailed as the savior of Moscow, whose numerically superior forces now bludgeoned their way toward the German capital. "They keep coming at us in hordes, wave after wave," reported a commander in the depleted German Ninth Army, mauled at Minsk the year before. "My men are fighting until they run out of ammunition," he added. "Then they are wiped out or completely overrun." To the south, Marshal Ivan Konev, commander of the First Ukrainian Front, shredded the Fourth Panzer Army before pivoting toward Berlin to compete with Zhukov for that prize. "Whoever reaches Berlin first," said Stalin, "let him take it." Zhukov had a shorter path to the city and won the race, but Konev's swift advance drew a noose around the capital.

On April 26, a half million Soviets launched a furious assault on central Berlin, site of the Reich Chancellery—under which lay Hitler's bombproof Führerbunker—and the nearby Reichstag, the old German parliament building, abandoned in 1933. Berlin's last-ditch defenders, including Waffen SS units and civilians of the Volkssturm, a people's militia made up largely of boys and old men, were outmanned and outgunned. But many fought to the bitter end in subway tunnels and streets as the city became a funeral pyre for the Reich and the leader who drove it to ruin. On April 30, Adolf Hitler committed suicide. That evening, Soviet troops fought their way into the Reichstag and raised their red flag over the smoldering capital. A week later, Grand Adm. Karl Dönitz, left in charge of the doomed Reich and its shattered armed forces, conceded defeat, and Germany surrendered unconditionally to the victorious Allies. ■

BELOW: **Soviets raise their flag over the Reichstag on May 2, two days after Hitler had committed suicide in his Führerbunker.**

Marines landed on Iwo Jima on February 19, 1945, but the scaling of Mount Suribachi took several days under heavy fire before the Stars and Stripes was raised on the 23rd. U.S. casualties reached 30,000.

CHAPTER 5

DEFEATING JAPAN

1943-1945

President Roosevelt signaled a fundamental shift in the war against Japan during his State of the Union address in early 1943. "Last year, we stopped them," said President Roosevelt of Japanese forces. "This year, we intend to advance."

Allied victories on Guadalcanal and Papua confirmed that Japanese gains in the Pacific had indeed been halted. In May 1943, the Joint Chiefs of Staff authorized a dual drive against Japan by General MacArthur and Adm. Chester Nimitz, the Pacific Fleet commander. Nimitz's sailors, naval airmen, and Marines were joined by Army troops in seizing fiercely defended islands, including bases on Tarawa and Makin Atolls in November 1943. Subsequent landings on Saipan, Tinian, and Guam allowed B-29s to begin blasting Japan in late 1944. U.S. naval forces supported MacArthur's soldiers as they took New Guinea and invaded the Philippine island of Leyte in October 1944. By this point in the long war of attrition in the Pacific theater, it was clear to Americans in every type of military uniform that the mindset of the enemy was to fight to the death. Island fighting intensified in February 1945, with the American invasion of Iwo Jima, where Lt. Gen. Tadamichi Kuribayashi vowed that every man would "resist until the end, making his position his tomb." By then, U.S. submarine attacks had stemmed the flow of oil and other vital supplies to Japan, and it faced dual threats—invasion by way of Okinawa and nuclear Armageddon as the top secret Manhattan Project achieved its explosive objective. Deliverance for Allied soldiers and defeat for their foes came in August after nuclear blasts devastated Hiroshima and Nagasaki, finally bringing an end to the war in the Pacific.

JUNE 21-30, 1943
Operation Cartwheel begins as Adm. William Halsey's U.S. Marines land on the Solomon Islands and General MacArthur's troops advance on New Guinea.

NOVEMBER 20, 1943
American forces land on Tarawa and Makin Atolls in the Gilbert Islands, the first steps in an advance across the central Pacific.

OCTOBER 20, 1944
MacArthur returns to the Philippines by landing with his troops on Leyte.

OCTOBER 23-26, 1944
U.S. fleets crush the Japanese Navy in the Battle of Leyte Gulf. Kamikaze attacks on U.S. warships begin.

FEBRUARY 19, 1945
U.S. Marines land on Iwo Jima.

MARCH 3, 1945
MacArthur's forces take Manila, but their efforts to secure Luzon and other Philippine islands will continue into the summer.

MARCH 9-10, 1945
B-29s fire-bomb Tokyo, devastating the Japanese capital.

APRIL 1, 1945
American troops invade Okinawa.

AUGUST 6-9, 1945
The U.S. drops an atomic bomb on Hiroshima, Japan, and three days later on Nagasaki.

SEPTEMBER 2, 1945
Japanese representatives formally surrender.

TWO PATHS TO TOKYO

++++++++++++

Officially, General MacArthur and Admiral Nimitz were partners in the drive against Japan, but they had their differences. MacArthur, having pledged to return to the Philippines, insisted that the road to Tokyo ran through Manila. Nimitz and Adm. Ernest King, chief of the U.S. Navy and Marine Corps, argued for island-hopping across the central Pacific until Japan was within striking range. MacArthur found naval support in Nimitz's commander in the South Pacific, Admiral Halsey, and they began a joint operation, called Cartwheel, in late June 1943. MacArthur arranged for Halsey, to cross into his operational zone above Guadalcanal and advance up the Solomon Island chain while MacArthur's troops pushed west along the north coast of New Guinea.

Marines and soldiers under Halsey's command landed on New Georgia and engaged in harrowing jungle warfare but seized crucial Japanese airstrips. By then, MacArthur's American and Australian forces had made similar gains on New Guinea, aided by Maj. Gen. George Kenney's Fifth Air Force.

"GENTLEMEN, WE WILL NOT NEUTRALIZE; WE WILL NOT DESTROY; WE WILL OBLITERATE THE DEFENSES.

—REAR ADM. HOWARD KINGMAN, PREPARING TO BOMBARD TARAWA ATOLL

LEFT: **General MacArthur sits between President Roosevelt and Admiral Nimitz in Honolulu in July 1944. The Navy closely supported MacArthur's advance toward the Philippines, though Nimitz continued to disagree over the quickest path to victory over Japan.** OPPOSITE: **Troops, trucks, and antiaircraft guns crowd a landing craft bound for Sansapor near New Guinea's western tip.**

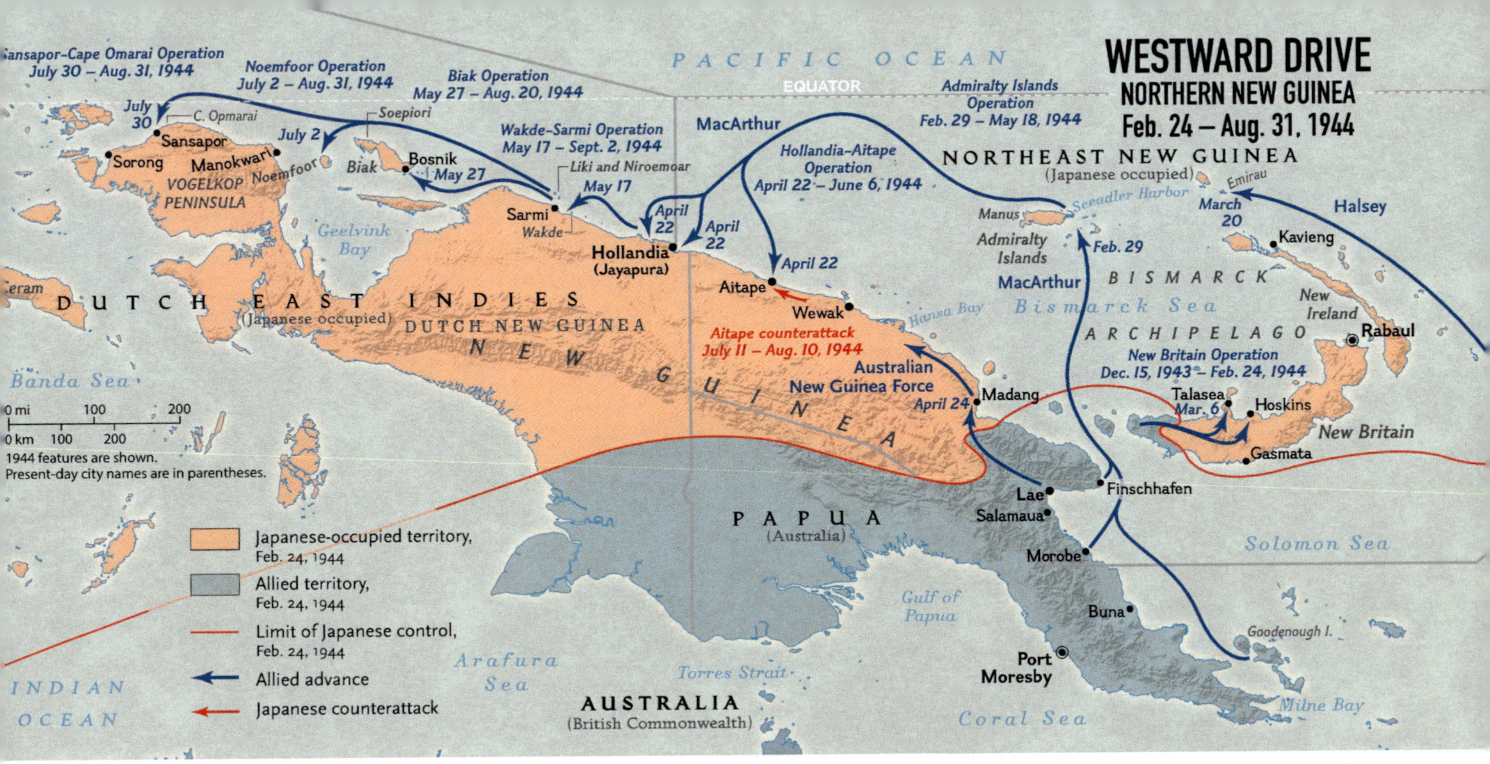

MacArthur's naval resources allowed him to advance by leaps and bounds along New Guinea's north coast and envelop Japanese troops.

Farther north, Nimitz's drive across the central Pacific began in the Gilbert Islands on November 20 with landings on Japanese-occupied islands within two atolls—Makin and Tarawa. The Marines suffered more than 3,000 casualties before securing Tarawa.

THE ROAD BACK

To return to the Philippines, MacArthur first had to oust Japan from New Guinea, one of the war's most forbidding battlegrounds. Yet, in January 1944, MacArthur had more than 1,000 miles (1,600 km) to go before reaching islands off western New Guinea.

After landing troops at Saidor in early January 1944, MacArthur invaded the Admiralty Islands in late February to seize Japanese airfields for Kenney's airmen. From the Admiralties, he sought out a foothold on the north coast of New Guinea, achieved when the port of Hollandia was captured in late April in Operation Reckless. Sturdy Australian troops grappled with the enemy inland while U.S. forces moved along the north coast. In May, MacArthur's forces secured Biak, a large coral island off northern New Guinea, before pursuing a westward drive up the Vogelkop Peninsula in July. Kenney's Fifth Air Force and Vice Adm. Thomas Kinkaid's Seventh Fleet supported their swift advances.

Many isolated Japanese units remained on New Guinea to be mopped up. That task was relegated to the Australians, who were left behind in October 1944, as MacArthur prepared to reclaim the Philippines.

WAR UNDER THE PACIFIC

By 1944, U.S. submarines in the Pacific were waging strategic warfare on a massive scale. Vice Adm. Charles Lockwood's submarine fleet in the southwest Pacific throttled Japan by severing its maritime supply lines, attacking vulnerable oil tankers and vessels carrying supplies on which Japan's war effort depended.

The versatile fleet simultaneously targeted troopships and warships, delivering special forces and underwater demolition teams to Pacific islands,

Maps printed on rayon were survival tools for downed airmen in rafts and guided rescuers operating off the shores of New Guinea. This chart shows the direction, steadiness, and speed of currents, and the direction and speed of prevailing winds, marked with broad arrows.

DOWNED PILOTS OFF THE NEW GUINEA COAST

Airmen of General Kenney's Fifth Air Force often conducted skip-bombing attacks at low level that left them vulnerable to armed ships. "Upon passing over the target, the element of surprise is lost," one pilot remarked, "so it is best to pull all the power you can and make a hurried departure." Bombers often returned to base "holed" by fire from Japanese guns. Provisions for the survival of Army or Navy airmen who crash-landed included maps printed on water-resistant cloth. The example above—produced by the U.S. Navy Hydrographic Office—shows the direction and velocity of currents and prevailing winds in winter months off the north coast of New Guinea. Downed airmen at sea equipped with inflatable rafts, paddles, and a compass could use such maps to navigate toward land. The maps also helped search-and-rescue personnel determine where survivors in rafts might be in relation to a crash site.

In February 1944, during a raid on the Japanese air and naval base at Kavieng, New Ireland, several planes crash-landed in Kavieng Harbor. Lt. Nathan Green Gordon, a Navy Catalina pilot, landed under fire, "picked up three men, saw two more clinging to a piece of debris, landed again, kept seeing more survivors, and kept on landing, until he had gone into that hornets' nest seven times." For saving 15 airmen, Gordon received the Medal of Honor.

rescuing downed Allied airmen, and reporting on enemy fleet movements.

Subs on patrol from newly established bases such as Milne Bay on New Guinea had sufficient range to enter the South China Sea and attack ships carrying oil and rubber from Burma and the Dutch East Indies before returning to base. Prowling the South China Sea aboard the sub U.S.S. *Jack* on February 19, 1944, Cmdr. Thomas Dykers targeted a convoy and sank four tankers carrying aviation fuel without enemy retaliation. "Needless to say," he said of his crew afterward, "morale is soaring."

TAKING THE MARIANAS

In June 1944, the U.S. Fifth Fleet in the Central Pacific Area bore down on the Japanese-occupied islands of Saipan, Tinian, and Guam in the Marianas, which would bring powerful B-29 bombers within range of Tokyo. Led by Vice Adm. Raymond Spruance, the massive fleet included 15 aircraft carriers and dozens of transports carrying 125,000 Marines and Army troops. Spruance's task was to guard their landings against attack by Vice Adm. Jisaburo Ozawa's First Mobile Fleet, which contained most of Japan's warships.

On June 15, Marines stormed Saipan, whose defenders were pounded relentlessly by the Fifth Fleet. Only Ozawa's intervention could save them, but a carrier task force dispatched by Spruance beat back the First Mobile Fleet in the Battle of the Philippine Sea on June 19–20. In early July, desperate Japanese soldiers launched a suicide attack and were decimated. Many civilians then threw themselves off cliffs rather than yield to Americans whom they believed would slaughter them.

In July, Marines and infantry invaded the islands of Guam and Tinian. Although Tinian was taken by August 1, die-hard Japanese troops would long hold out there and on Guam, where the defeated Japanese commander, Lt. Gen. Hideyoshi Obata, committed suicide on August 11. Seizing the Marianas cost more than 25,000 American casualties, but the impact on Japan was huge. Emperor Hirohito had warned that if Saipan fell, "air attacks on Tokyo will follow." His fears were soon realized. ■

BELOW: **Standing by a Grumman Hellcat, Lt. Alexander Vraciu holds up six fingers for the planes he downed during the "Great Marianas Turkey Shoot." U.S. pilots downed nearly 300 Japanese aircraft while losing about 30 planes.**

CHINA-BURMA-INDIA

++++++++++++++

Intent on keeping a tight hold on China, Japanese chiefs kept nearly a million troops stationed there while their forces in the Pacific were stretched thin and lost ground to the Allied advances of late 1943 and early 1944. Japanese troops controlled eastern China, but Chiang Kai-shek's Nationalist forces held out at Kunming, not far from Burma; Chiang's Nationalist Party had splintered between ousting the invading Japanese and fighting the internal communist threat. Japan had invaded Burma in early 1942 to cut off vital supplies to the Nationalists and keep Allied troops at bay, but American airmen continued to operate in China against the Japanese. The Flying Tigers of the American Volunteer Group—organized to support Chinese Nationalists before the United States entered the war—formed the nucleus of the 23rd Fighter Group, which in 1943 became part of the U.S. 14th Army Air Force, based at Kunming and led by Maj. Gen. Claire Chennault, founder of the Flying Tigers. As he prepared to bomb distant Japanese targets, pilots of the Air Transport Command flew troops and supplies over the mountainous "Hump" between British India and China—perilous flights that claimed the lives of 1,000 airmen by the war's end.

Lt. Gen. Joseph Stilwell, the U.S. Army commander in the theater designated CBI (China-Burma-India) and Chiang's chief of staff, proposed invading northern Burma and restoring the overland supply line between India and China that was severed when the Japanese closed the Burma Road. Stilwell called on American-trained Chinese units to enter Burma and fight in

MAY 12–25, 1943
Allied leaders authorize an offensive in northern Burma and a bombing campaign in China.

AUGUST 31, 1943
The OSS Detachment 101 recruits Kachin warriors to serve as guerrillas behind Japanese lines in Burma.

MARCH 8, 1944
Japanese Gen. Renya Mutaguchi launches a costly offensive from Burma into India, where his forces will falter under pressure and withdraw in July.

AUGUST 3, 1944
Stilwell's troops capture Myitkyina in northern Burma, clearing the way for supplies from India to reach Chinese Nationalists at Kunming on the Ledo and Burma Roads.

MAY 3, 1945
British forces recapture the Burmese capital, Rangoon.

conjunction with Merrill's Marauders, led by the American Brig. Gen. Frank Merrill. The Marauders, a U.S. Army special operations jungle warfare unit, emulated commandos from India called Chindits. The Chindits were organized by British Brig. Gen. Orde Wingate, who pioneered operations behind enemy lines in Burma. Stilwell's forces would be aided by Chindits as well as Kachin warriors, armed and instructed by agents of OSS Detachment 101 (see sidebar p. 100). Stilwell's arduous campaign, conducted in dense jungle, would help set the stage for a larger Allied offensive that ultimately broke Japan's grip on Burma.

THE FIGHT TO RECLAIM BURMA

Merrill's Marauders included veterans of Pacific campaigns with a knack for jungle warfare. Orde Wingate,

ABOVE: **Supply trucks could finally cross from India to China when the Stilwell Road was completed in 1945. A section in Guizhou, China, includes a spectacular 24 curves.**

the British Chindit commander, trained his troops for the upcoming operation behind Japanese lines in central Burma and was livid when Stilwell claimed those Marauders for his own campaign. Stilwell could "take his Americans and stick 'em," Wingate swore. Such disputes were common in CBI because resources were limited. Stilwell resented Chennault's 14th Air Force for hogging supplies flown over the Hump from India. By seizing Myitkyina and its nearby airfield—which Japanese fighter pilots used to attack those flights—Stilwell would boost supply deliveries by road and air to Nationalist troops in China and keep Japanese troops tied down there.

As it turned out, Wingate's operation aided Stilwell's campaign, which began in early 1944. In March, Chindits landed in gliders at a jungle clearing called Broadway. Joined by others arriving overland, they tore up tracks and waged guerrilla warfare, preventing Japanese reinforcements from reaching Myitkyina. Wingate died in a plane crash in late March, but the Indian Chindits continued to support Stilwell's troops, including his X Force (Chinese troops based in India as opposed to

ABOVE: **Members of the 23rd Fighter Group, organized in 1942, wore a shoulder patch featuring a winged tiger in honor of the original Flying Tigers of the American Volunteer Group.**

DETACHMENT 101: BEHIND ENEMY LINES

Organized secretly by the OSS (Office of Strategic Services), in 1942, Detachment 101 was led by Capt. Carl Eifler, a former U.S. Customs officer. When he reported to work under Lt. Gen. Joseph Stilwell, he was told to begin sabotaging Japanese supply lines in Burma within 90 days. "All I want to hear," Stilwell said, "is booms coming out of the jungle." Eifler and his OSS officers began training agents in India, including refugees who had fled the Japanese invasion of Burma. Recruits were assured that if they died in action, their next of kin would be compensated.

Impressed by the courage and stamina of Kachin warriors in northern Burma who were aiding the British, Eifler sent OSS Capt. Vincent Curl in late August 1943 to establish a base among them near Myitkyina, the objective of Stilwell's forthcoming offensive. Curl won the confidence of a Kachin chief named Zhing Htaw Naw, who was suffering from malaria, by reviving him with quinine. The chief agreed to supply hundreds of men who would be trained by the OSS. Soon Kachins were sabotaging bridges and rail lines and ambushing the enemy. Their intimate knowledge of the jungle and ability to spy on the Japanese undetected enabled OSS officers to draw detailed maps of areas where foes were active (see an example on the opposite page). Detachment 101 established command posts to direct the guerrilla warfare.

Kachin troops enlisted by the OSS

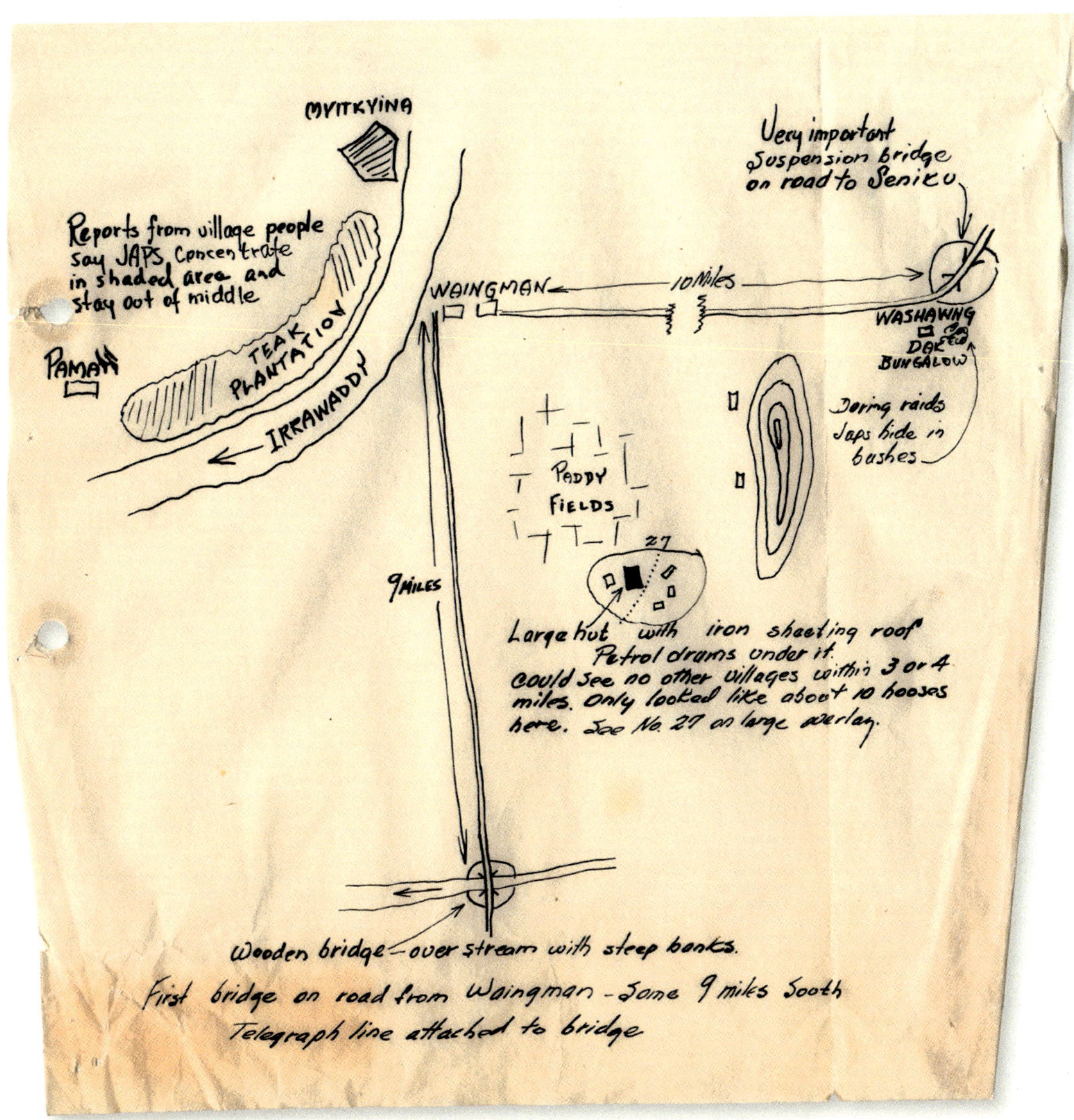

Close surveillance contributed to this hand-drawn OSS map, which notes that "during raids Japs hide in bushes" near a suspension bridge.

the Y Force in China) and Merrill's Marauders. Advancing toward Myitkyina on parallel tracks with the help of Detachment 101 and its Kachin recruits, they suffered as much from tropical diseases as from battle wounds. Monsoon rains made things worse, but Marauders rallied and seized the Myitkyina airstrip on May 16. That brought Stilwell enough aid to besiege the town and finally take it in early August. "Myitkyina over at last," he wrote. "Thank God."

Meanwhile, Japanese forces led by Lt. Gen. Renya Mutaguchi had invaded India, where Mutaguchi hoped to trigger a rebellion against British rule. But Indian forces under Lt. Gen. William Slim did not greet the Japanese as liberators and withstood sieges alongside British troops at Kohima and Imphal, where Slim flew in fresh units and supplies and forced the invaders to withdraw. Combined with the loss of Myitkyina, Mutaguchi's defeat weakened Japan's hold on Burma, which Allied forces reclaimed in an offensive beginning in late 1944. The only Japanese gains came in China, where they captured air bases of the U.S. 14th Air Force, reducing its range. That did not stop Americans from launching strategic bombers from newly acquired Pacific bases closer to Japan, which was edging closer to invasion or atomic destruction while many of its troops remained bogged down in China. ■

RETURN TO THE PHILIPPINES

+++++++++++++

In September 1944, MacArthur made his promised return to the Philippines, which witnessed his retreat in March 1942. More than 100,000 troops invaded Leyte on the first day, a huge challenge that involved coordinating shipments of men and equipment escorted by warships. To supplement the modest Seventh Fleet, Admiral Nimitz assigned Halsey's powerful Third Fleet to guard Leyte Gulf, through which invasion forces and any menacing Japanese warships would pass. The navy faced an all-out attack by Japanese Vice Adm. Takeo Kurita while a diversionary attack force lured Halsey's carriers to the north (see map opposite). When the complex offensive faltered for lack of coordination, U.S. forces began to shred the superbattleships of the Japanese Navy. Heroic efforts by airmen saved the American beachheads on Leyte.

Army divisions under Lt. Gen. Walter Krueger captured airstrips on the east coast of Leyte before meeting fierce resistance at "Breakneck Ridge," a treacherous pass along the west coast, where Japanese reinforcements were landing. Not until late December—after Krueger's 77th Infantry Division secured Ormoc—could MacArthur declare victory and target Luzon. The battles for Luzon and Manila proved costly for all concerned. MacArthur suffered more than 30,000 casualties on Luzon as he faced entrenched Japanese who terrorized civilians in war-torn Manila, where nearly 100,000 would perish. Filipino guerrillas and civilians supported American troops, trusting that the U.S. would soon fulfill its pledge to grant their country independence. The campaign did not lead directly to victory but nullified enemy forces that might have prolonged the war. ■

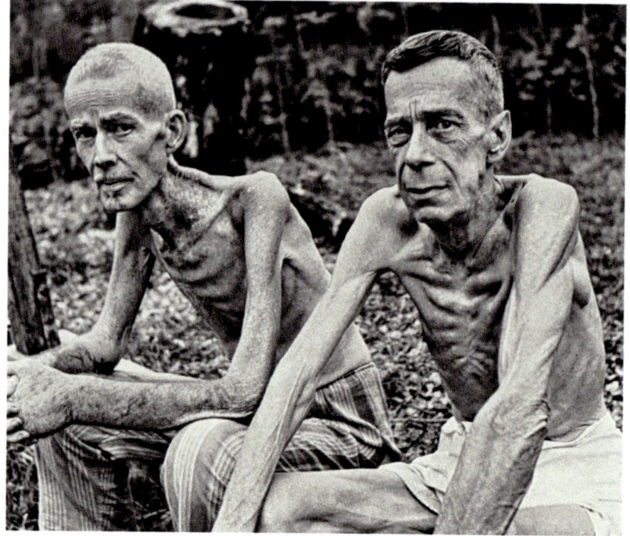

LEFT: **After three years of ill treatment by their Japanese captors, Americans Lee Rogers (left) and John Todd (right) were liberated by U.S. troops who entered Manila in February 1945.**

Vice Adm. Takeo Kurita devised a three-pronged offensive strategy to defend Leyte Gulf. However, his forces remained divided and were soundly defeated by Halsey's Third Fleet and by Seventh Fleet forces under Rear Admirals Jesse Oldendorf and Clifton Sprague.

CLOSING IN ON JAPAN

++++++++++++

Assigned in January 1945 to take charge of the 21st Bomber Command, which targeted Japan from bases on Saipan, Tinian, and Guam in long-range B-29s, Maj. Gen. Curtis LeMay noted that those big bombers had not yet "made much of a splash in the war." Flying at 30,000 feet (9,100 m), above the range of antiaircraft guns, they were buffeted by the jet stream, seldom bombed with much precision, and remained vulnerable to enemy fighters, which sometimes shot them down or rammed them in suicide attacks. Applying tactics used against Germany, LeMay planned to fire-bomb Tokyo and other Japanese cities at night from lower altitude. Worries that airmen might "get the holy hell shot out of us," as one of them put it, failed to deter the hard-driving general. But he urged the Navy and Marine Corps to proceed with a perilous invasion of Iwo Jima to seize enemy air bases there, which could then be used to provide B-29s with fighter escorts for attacks on Japan (see map opposite).

IWO JIMA AND THE LONG ROAD TO TOKYO

The landings on Iwo Jima in February and the fire-bombings that began on mainland Japan in March marked the final phase of the Pacific war, during which that brutal struggle became even crueler and deadlier. U.S. Navy planners hoped that sustained preliminary air and naval bombardments would allow Marines to capture Iwo Jima within a matter of days. However, when they landed on February 19, 1945, their progress proved painfully slow. The Americans soon came under lethal fire from nearby Mount Suribachi, and it took Marines several days to fight their way up that peak—atop which they famously raised the Stars and Stripes on the 23rd (see photo on page 92)—and more than a month to secure the island and its airfields at a cost of some 30,000 casualties.

LEFT: **The sight of snowcapped Mount Fuji told American airmen in B-29s that they were approaching Tokyo.**

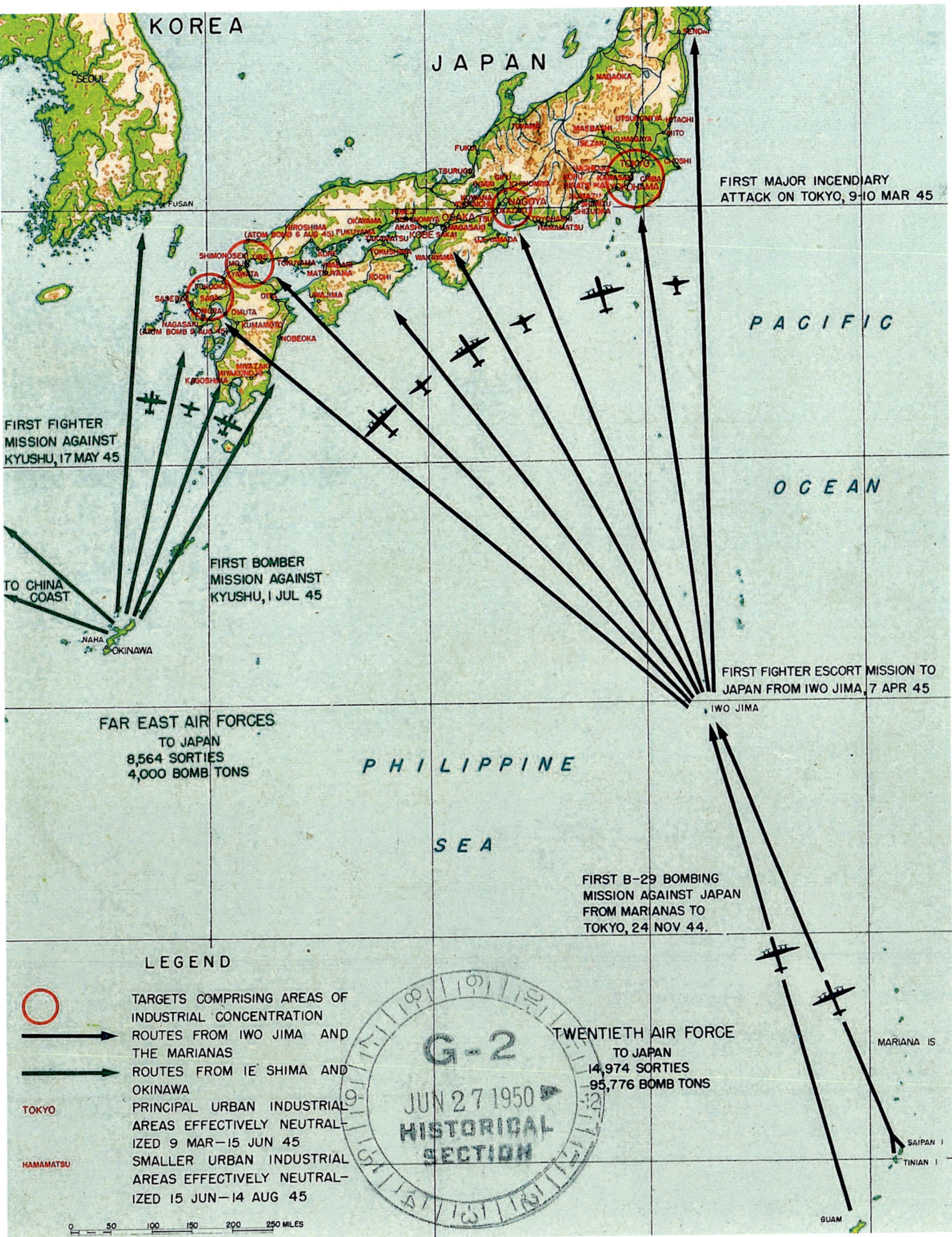

This map shows the strategic value of hard-fought Iwo Jima, where air bases launched long-range B-29 bombers (shown as large planes with four engines), which were escorted to Japan by shorter-range fighters (small planes).

The Japanese soldiers fighting under Lt. Gen. Tadamichi Kuribayashi at Iwo Jima heeded his order to resist to the end, making their position their tomb. He hoped their sacrifice would delay "enemy air raids on Tokyo." By the time he committed suicide on Iwo Jima in late March, however, much of Tokyo had been incinerated. Yet, neither the inferno that killed more than 80,000 people in Tokyo on the night of March 9 nor subsequent fire-bombings induced the Japanese to surrender. Plans to invade proceeded, beginning in April with a costly assault on Okinawa, the staging area for an attack on Japan's home islands. The bloodbath at Okinawa foretold huge casualties if U.S. troops had to fight their way to Tokyo.

SECRET PLANS TO INVADE JAPAN

The death of President Roosevelt on April 12, 1945, left his successor, Harry S. Truman, responsible for defeating Japan. Truman was also informed of the secret plan to invade Japan, designated Operation Downfall. That massive offensive, aimed first at the island of Kyushu and ultimately at the main island of Honshu, would involve several million soldiers, sailors, and airmen. The Japanese planned to fight to the death by using some 10,000 remaining aircraft for kamikaze attacks on American forces and enlisting all male civilians from 15 to 60 and all women from 17 to 40 as home guards, armed with firearms or bamboo spears. It was estimated that as many as a million Americans and several times as many Japanese might be killed or wounded before the struggle ended. After taking the oath of office, Truman was told that the U.S. was secretly developing atomic bombs of enormous power. There was no assurance that using them would vanquish Japan, but it offered another option. As commander in chief, Truman felt obligated to minimize American casualties, and he was ready to use nuclear weapons to that end. The first use of the atomic bomb was not a decision that Truman and his advisers took without great deliberation on its implications for the future of mankind: "It is an awful responsibility that has come to us," the president wrote. ■

BELOW: **The U.S. Navy suffered more than 10,000 casualties off Okinawa as a result of kamikaze attacks on ships like this one on the aircraft carrier U.S.S. *Bunker Hill*.**

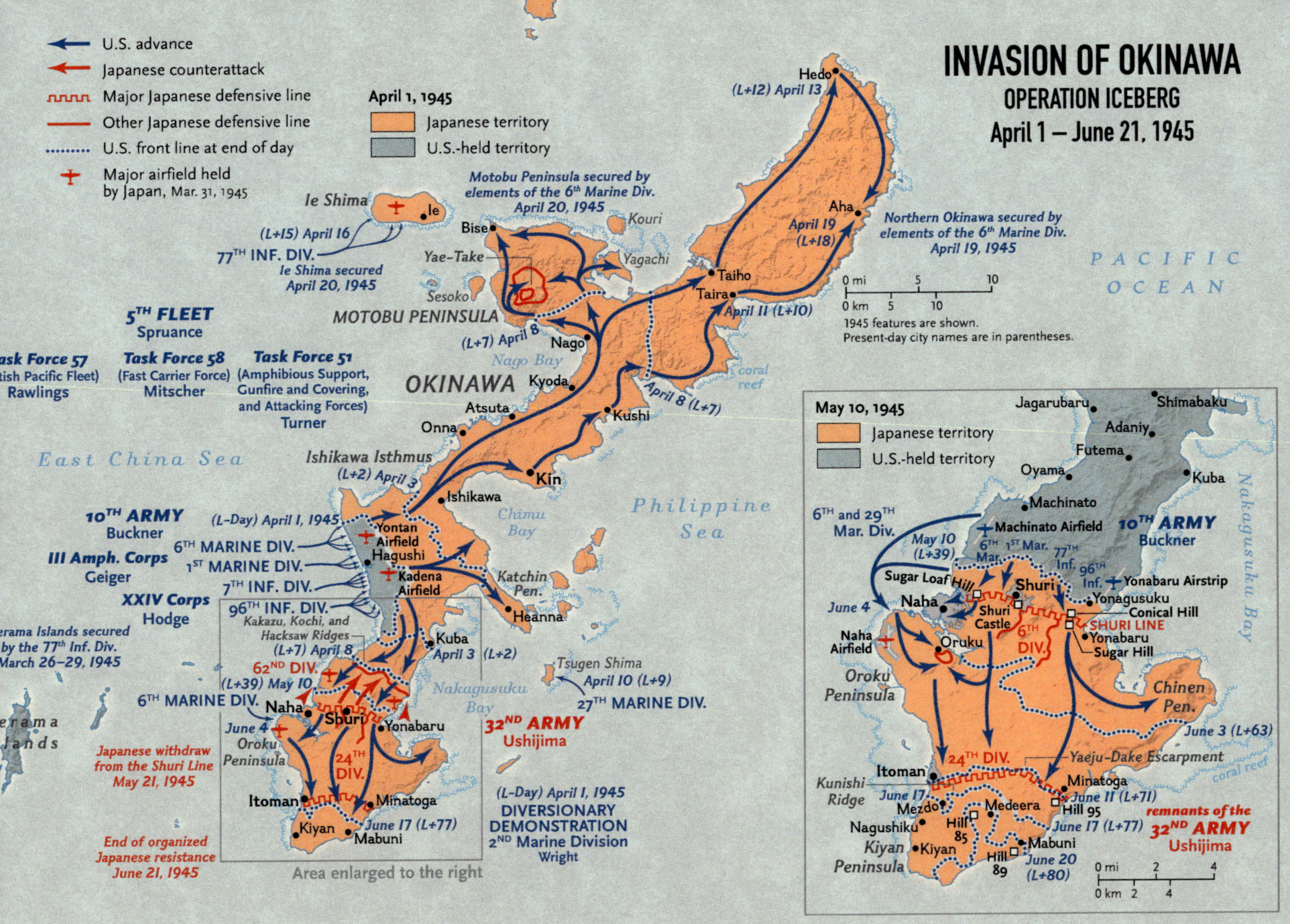

Marines feigned a landing on Okinawa's south coast on April 1, 1945, while the actual invasion took place on the west coast by Marine and infantry divisions of Buckner's 10th Army. His forces had to overcome two defensive lines before Ushijima's troops withdrew southward from Shuri to their last line of defense (inset map).

OKINAWA: ORDEAL BY LAND AND SEA

The struggle for Okinawa offered a grim preview of a potential U.S. invasion of Japan. Many of Okinawa's 450,000 inhabitants were conscripted to defend the island. Including Okinawans and troops of his 32nd Army, Lt. Gen. Mitsuru Ushijima had more than 100,000 men. His defensive lines crossed a narrow part of the island in the south (see map above), where ridges laced with caves and tunnels offered cover. Headquartered at Shuri Castle in Okinawa's capital, Ushijima allowed the U.S. 10th Army under Lt. Gen. Simon Bolivar Buckner, Jr., to land uncontested north of Shuri on April 1, 1945, and awaited an attack.

The Japanese launched suicide attacks on the Fifth Fleet's Task Force 58 that was shielding Buckner's offensive. The superbattleship I.J.N. *Yamato* was sunk by carrier-based warplanes before it could enter battle. Most Japanese planes were shot down before they struck targets, but kamikazes sank nearly 30 American ships and killed or wounded thousands of sailors.

Outnumbered nearly two to one, Ushijima's troops fought tenaciously against the Americans, who had to claw their way up muddy slopes strewn with dead bodies. As one Marine recalled, it was like being "flung into hell's own cesspool." In late May, Ushijima withdrew and opted for suicide. Buckner was killed by Japanese shell fire on June 18. Victory cost Americans more than 50,000 casualties. At least 150,000 Japanese troops and Okinawans died, including many civilians.

BOMBING HIROSHIMA AND NAGASAKI

+++++++++++++

When Harry S. Truman assumed the presidency of the United States, the Nazi Reich of Adolf Hitler was all but defeated in Europe. This meant that Truman's main responsibility was the defeat of Japan in the Pacific theater. He was also mindful of the ongoing loss of American lives and the growing depletion of military resources, which were spread thin after four years of war across three continents.

However, in the spring of 1945, the successful culmination of the top secret Manhattan Project gave the new president the option to employ atomic weaponry for the first time in history. While contemplating such a historic step, Truman and his advisers weighed the awful impact that the bomb would have on the civilian population of Japan against the lives it might save by ending the war quickly. An immediate and decisive conclusion would prevent prolonged battles all the way to Tokyo.

Soon after arriving at Potsdam, Germany, in mid-July to confer with Allied leaders, Truman learned that an atomic bomb had been successfully tested in the New Mexico desert. He informed Stalin that the U.S. had developed a "new weapon of unusual destructive force," which might be used against Japan. Stalin had already been informed of the bomb by Soviet spies and was preparing to join the war in Asia by invading Japanese-occupied Manchuria. On July 26, Allied leaders issued the Potsdam Declaration, calling on Japan to surrender unconditionally or face "prompt and utter destruction." Truman included in the declaration a pledge to remove Allied occupation forces from Japan once a "peacefully inclined and responsible government" was established. But he rejected language that would have allowed Emperor Hirohito, Japan's commander in chief, to remain in power. Japanese leaders refused to yield, triggering their nation's downfall.

> MY GOD, WHAT HAVE WE DONE?
>
> —CAPT. ROBERT LEWIS, CO-PILOT OF THE *ENOLA GAY*, OVER HIROSHIMA

LEFT: **The blast that shattered Hiroshima stopped the clock shown here at the precise time of impact, 8:16 a.m.**

As documented by two photos (below right) taken before and after an atomic bomb exploded above a stadium in Nagasaki on August 9, little was left standing within a few thousand yards of ground zero. People close to the blast, which produced the mushroom cloud (above), were vaporized. Others farther from ground zero (below left) suffered burns and other injuries that often proved fatal.

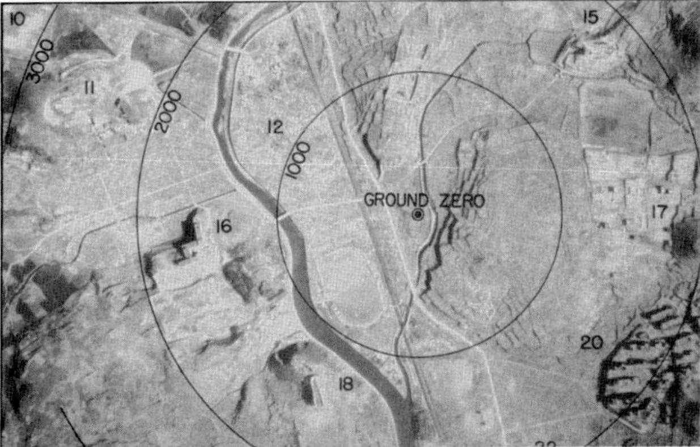

FATEFUL FLIGHTS

Several cities including Tokyo, Nagoya, and Osaka had all been heavily fire-bombed by the time the new weapons were perfected and thus were ruled out as targets. Five other cities were spared strategic bombing in early 1945 to serve as possible targets for nuclear weapons—Niigata, Kyoto, Hiroshima, Kokura, and Nagasaki. Secretary of War Henry Stimson ruled out bombing Kyoto, the historical heart of Japan. Hiroshima was the primary target when Col. Paul Tibbets and crew took off from Tinian before dawn on August 6, 1945, in a B-29 carrying an atomic bomb fueled with uranium-235. At daybreak, a weather plane reported clear skies over Hiroshima, and Tibbets received the go-ahead. At 8:16 a.m., the bomb detonated, destroying much of the city and killing more than 100,000 people directly, a death toll that later increased as those sickened by radiation died. The blast that shattered Hiroshima produced a mushroom cloud that pilot Tibbets described as "terrible and incredibly tall." His co-pilot, Capt. Robert Lewis, reacted to the blast below exclaiming, "My God, what have we done?"

In the early hours of August 9, Soviet troops invaded Manchuria. Around the same time, a B-29 piloted by Maj. Charles Sweeney left Tinian carrying a bomb fueled with plutonium-239. The primary target was Kokura, site of a major arsenal, but smoke obscured the target there. Low on fuel, Sweeney decided to strike Nagasaki and refuel on Okinawa. Cloud cover prevented the bomb from being dropped precisely, but it killed approximately 40,000 people and doomed many others to sickness and death. On August 15, Hirohito announced that Japan would yield to prevent its "ultimate collapse and obliteration." Japanese officers formally surrendered on September 2 in Tokyo Bay aboard the battleship *Missouri,* which had been targeted by a kamikaze earlier that year. A catastrophic world war that had claimed the lives of more than 20 million combatants and at least 30 million civilians was finally over. "The next war might destroy the world," wrote Gen. George Marshall. "It must not come." ■

BELOW: **Mamoru Shigemitsu signs the Japanese surrender aboard the U.S.S. *Missouri* in Tokyo Bay.** OPPOSITE: **The good news reaches Chicago on Wednesday, August 15, 1945.**

3¢ DAILY TIMES

CHICAGO'S PICTURE NEWSPAPER

Copyright, 1945, by Chicago TIMES, Inc.

Vol. 16, No. 341 | DEA. 2323 | WEDNESDAY, AUGUST 15, 1945 | 40 Pages

NIGHT EXTRA

JULY Daily Average Net Paid Sales

452,246

94% CIRCULATION IN THE CITY AND SUBURBS

PEACE

Isn't it wonderful?

END GAS RATION

MAC'S 1ST ORDERS TO HIRO

Stories begin on page 2

ATLAS OF WORLD WAR II

PRODUCED BY NATIONAL GEOGRAPHIC PARTNERS, LLC
1145 17th Street NW
Washington, DC 20036-4688 USA

Material in this publication is drawn from the National Geographic book *Atlas of World War II.*

ISSN 2160-7141

Published by Meredith Corporation
225 Liberty Street • New York, NY 10281

Printed in the USA

Special thanks to Justin Kavanagh, Elisa Gibson, David Rogowski, Moriah Petty, Bridget Hamilton, Susan Blair, Jill Foley, Matt Propert, and Michael O'Connor.

ILLUSTRATIONS CREDITS

Cover, NG Maps; 0-1, Hulton Archive/Getty Images; 2-3, Underwood Archives/Getty Images; 4-5, NG Maps; 6-7, Image courtesy of U.S. Naval Academy Museum; 8, ullstein bild/ullstein bild via Getty Images; 10, Hilary Jane Morgan/Getty Images; 12, Bettmann/Getty Images; 15, Hulton-Deutsch Collection/CORBIS/Corbis via Getty Images; 17 (UP), akg-images; 17 (LO), Courtesy Imperial War Museum, Neg. #4394; 18, Bert Hardy/Keystone/Getty Images; 21, Kenneth W. Rendell, The International Museum of World War II; 22 (UP), Keystone/Getty Images; 22 (LO), Topical Press Agency/Getty Images; 23, Daily Mirror/Mirrorpix/Mirrorpix via Getty Images; 24, AP Photo/File; 26, Kenneth W. Rendell, The International Museum of World War II; 27, WWII Aerial Photos and Maps, www.wwii-photos-maps.com; 28, Keystone-France/Gamma-Keystone via Getty Images; 30, ullstein bild/ullstein bild via Getty Images; 31, Stanford University Libraries; 32, Kenneth W. Rendell, The International Museum of World War II; 34, From *Reports of General MacArthur,* vol. II, pt. 1 (Department of the Army, 1966), p. 69; 35 (UP), US Signal Corps/US Signal Corps/The LIFE Picture Collection/Getty Images; 35 (LO), Henry Groskinsky/The LIFE Images Collection/Getty Images; 37, Japanese American National Museum (Gift of A. Iwata, 97.194.4); 40, U.S. Naval History and Heritage Command Photograph; 41, U.S. National Archives; 42, Hulton Archive/Getty Images; 44, Kenneth W. Rendell, The International Museum of World War II; 45, George Silk/The LIFE Picture Collection/Getty Images; 47 (BOTH), Kenneth W. Rendell, The International Museum of World War II; 48, Hulton Archive/Getty Images; 50, U.S. Air Force; 54, ullstein bild/ullstein bild via Getty Images; 55 (UP), ullstein bild/ullstein bild via Getty Images; 55 (LO), Kenneth W. Rendell, The International Museum of World War II; 56, Universal History Archive/UIG via Getty Images; 58, ullstein bild/ullstein bild via Getty Images; 61, AP Photo/U.S. Army Signal Corps; 62, Kenneth W. Rendell, The International Museum of World War II; 64, Trinity Mirror/Mirrorpix/Alamy Stock Photo; 65, Walter Hahn, Dresden © akg-images/The Image Works; 69, Roger Viollet/Getty Images; 70, Kenneth W. Rendell, The International Museum of World War II; 71, Sovfoto/UIG via Getty Image; 72, Art Media/Print Collector/Getty Images; 74, U.S. Coast Guard Collection/U.S. National Archives; 77 (UP), Kenneth W. Rendell, The International Museum of World War II; 77 (LO), Prisma by Dukas Presseagentur GmbH/Alamy Stock Photo; 79, U.S. National Archives; 80, Bettmann/Getty Images; 81, Popperfoto/Getty Images; 82, Bob Landry/The LIFE Images Collection/Getty Images; 83, Kenneth W. Rendell, The International Museum of World War II; 86, AFP/Getty Images; 87 (ALL), Library of Congress, Geography and Map Division; 88, AP Photo/U.S. Army; 91, © Khaldei/Voller Ernst/akg-images; 92, U.S. National Archives; 94, Hulton Archive/Getty Images; 95 (LO), US Coast Guard/Getty Images; 96, Kenneth W. Rendell, The International Museum of World War II; 97, U.S. National Archives; 99, U.S. National Archives; 100 (UP), Private Collection/© Don Troiani/Bridgeman Images; 100 (LO), Keystone/Hulton Archive/Getty Images; 101, U.S. National Archives; 102, Carl Mydans/The LIFE Picture Collection/Getty Images; 104, Bettmann/Getty Images; 105, U.S. National Archives; 106, Roger Viollet/Getty Images; 108, Brian Brake/Science Source; 109 (UP), Universal History Archive/UIG via Getty Images; 109 (LO LE), ADN-Bildarchiv/ullstein bild via Getty Images; 109 (CTR RT and LO RT), MPI/Getty Images; 110, akg-images; 111, Library of Congress, 0068a-7s; 113, Universal History Archive/UIG via Getty Images.

OPPOSITE: **Adolf Hitler stands before the Eiffel Tower in Paris soon after France surrendered in June 1940.**

Made in the USA
Middletown, DE
11 April 2021